# VIRGINIA SUPPLEMENT FOR
# Modern Real Estate Practice

**JOHN M. WARE**
**JAMES L. WINDSOR**

**REAL ESTATE EDUCATION COMPANY**
® a division of Longman Financial Services Institute, Inc.

While a great deal of care has been taken to provide accurate and current information, the ideas, suggestions, general principles, and conclusions presented in this book are subject to local, state, and federal laws and regulations, court cases, and any revisions of same. The reader is thus urged to consult legal counsel regarding any points of law--this publication should not be used as a substitute for competent legal advice.

ISBN: 0-88462-880-9

Printed in the United States of America.

89  90  91  10  9  8  7  6  5  4  3  2  1

**Library of Congress Cataloging-in-Publication Data**

Ware, John (John M.)
      Virginia supplement for Modern real estate practice  /  John Ware,
James Windsor.
            p.    cm.
      Includes index.
      ISBN 0-88462-880-9
      1.    Real estate business--Law and legislation--Virginia.
2.  Vendors and purchasers--Virginia. 3.  Real property--Virginia.
4.  Real estate business--Virginia. I.  Windsor, James. II.  Galaty,
Fillmore W.  Modern real estate practice. III.  Title. IV.  Title:
Modern real estate practice.
KF2042.R4G34  1988 Suppl. 4
346.7304'37--dc20
[347.306437]
                                                                89-10153
                                                                CIP

# Contents

# Preface

The profession of real estate in the Commonwealth of Virginia is affected by customs, practices and usages that have evolved within the state and particular localities, as well as the specific statutory provisions passed by the Virginia legislature and embodied in the Regulations of the Real Estate Board (REB). Persons who want to practice real estate in Virginia must be aware of all the applicable laws and regulations prior to licensure and of changes that affect them as new laws and regulations are made.

This supplement has two primary purposes: to aid the student in preparing for the Virginia licensing examination (salesperson or broker) and to supply in layman's terms a summary and reference book on Virginia law as it applies to real estate.

This book is designed as a supplement to *Modern Real Estate Practice* by Galaty, Allaway and Kyle, published by Real Estate Education Company. Wherever possible, any duplication of material covered in *Modern Real Estate Practice* has been avoided in the present work; further, it is assumed that the student has already mastered the main text before reading the supplement (though the two may be used concurrently). Chapter numbers in the supplement correspond to those in the main text; this means that certain chapters have been omitted in the supplement where subject matter in the main text is general or national in scope and Virginia law offers nothing that varies from or speaks to information in the main text.

Each chapter in the supplement is followed by questions in exam format, with answers and (where deemed necessary) explanations. In those chapters dealing with Virginia license law and certain other topics, citations have been made of the sources in Virginia code or the REB Regulations to which the student may refer in researching particular issues.

Although this supplement is intended to help the student pass the licensing examination, it is the authors' aim to give students as comprehensive an overview as possible of the Virginia laws that actually affect their potential practice in real estate. Thus the supplement embodies the Virginia license law in its entirety, either by direct quotation or paraphrase, so that the student may understand his obligations regarding ethics and competence in the field. In addition, aspects of Virginia law besides license law, issues such as riparian rights, mechanics' liens, marital rights in property, or statute and case law, are dealt with in greater depth in the supplement than in the main text. While many aspects of Virginia law may never be tested on a licensing exam, they will certainly be encountered in the field, where knowledge of the law is most effective when it does not have to be learned after the fact. Needless to say, should a legal problem arise regarding any issue dealt with in the text, licensees should seek competent legal advice rather than deal with the problem themselves.

In using this book as a preparation aid for the Virginia licensing examination, the student should take advantage of the many questions supplied in the same format as the examinations administered by Virginia's examination vendor, Assessment Systems Inc. At the same time, none of the questions in this book, to the authors' knowledge, is an actual examination question; the REB Regulations specifically forbid the use of actual examination questions. The questions are intended to test the student's knowledge and help him or her broaden and deepen that knowledge, so that test questions on the licensing examination will address concepts the student is familiar with through comprehensive and thorough study. "A little knowledge is a dangerous thing." In the practice of real estate this statement is especially true: the student who passes the licensing examination merely from being coached through hundreds of examination questions does not, in fact, know real estate; he or she will be operating in the field in ignorance and will likely end up--possibly with the principal broker of the firm--in deep trouble. The present supplement is designed to foster the comprehensive knowledge that can help to insure competent performance in the field. A note on English grammar as employed by the authors: In contexts where (for example) the broker is the subject, in later references the generic pronoun he is employed rather than the cumbersome he or she. This traditional approach to grammar implies no insensitivity to fairness issues.

The authors wish to extend sincere thanks for permission to use the forms reproduced in this text: the Massanutten Board of Realtors, for the listing form in Chapter 6; and Southgate Mortgage Corporation of Virginia Beach, for the deed of trust in Chapter 15.

Further, we wish to thank the many people who have given help in this project: Christina Meier, attorney for GSH Residential Real Estate Corporation, Virginia Beach; and Richard Hagle, Margaret Maloney and Thomas Sharpe of Real Estate Education Company. Thanks are also due to the experts who read the manuscript and gave excellent suggestions during its preparation: Andy Piplico of Piplico and Associates, Williamsburg; George Rink, director of the Mount Vernon Academy, Alexandria; and Paul Hartman, instructor of marketing education, Arlington Public Schools.

## ABOUT THE AUTHORS

John M. Ware is manager of the Principles School of GSH Residential Real Estate Corporation of Virginia Beach. He is a member of the Real Estate Educators Association, has sold real estate as an active licensee since 1982 and has taught real estate since 1985. He was one of the reviewers who assisted in preparing the 11th edition of *Modern Real Estate Practice*. He holds the Associate Broker license in Virginia. Dr. Ware has earned a Ph.D. degree in music history and is an active composer, performer and reviewer of music in addition to his real estate activity.

James L. Windsor is a practicing attorney at law with the prominent law firm Kaufman and Canoles, where he is a member of the Real Estate Finance Team. An honor graduate of James Madison University, Mr. Windsor holds a Juris Doctor degree from the T. C. Williams School of Law of the University of Richmond. He is a member of the Virginia Bar Association and the Virginia State Bar. He is well-known as a lecturer on a variety of real estate and legal topics.

# 5

# Real Estate Brokerage

## DEFINITIONS

In Virginia, a real estate **broker** is defined as "any person, partnership, association, or corporation who, for a compensation or a valuable consideration, *sells* or offers for sale, *buys* or offers to buy, or *negotiates* the purchase or sale or exchange of real estate, including units or interests in condominiums, cooperative interest...or time shares in a time-share program...or who *leases* or offers to lease, or *rents* or offers for rent, any real estate or the improvements thereon for others, as a whole or partial vocation" (see Va. Code 54-730, Cum. Supp. 1987).

The same definition applies to a real estate salesperson, except that the salesperson is retained either directly as an employee or indirectly as an independent contractor by a real estate broker. The salesperson is an **agent** of the broker and, in acting for any of the broker's clients, a **subagent** to the client.

The word *broker* as used above refers to the firm transacting real estate business. Individuals may also hold broker's licenses and may be distinguished according to function as follows:

The **principal broker** is the individual designated by the firm to bear responsibility for the activities of the firm and all its licensees and to receive correspondence from the Real Estate Board.

The **supervising broker** (known as a managing broker in some contexts) is an individual holding a broker's license who has been designated by the firm to supervise the activities of a branch office.

An **associate broker** is any individual other than the principal broker who holds a broker's license. Supervising brokers are associate brokers. An associate broker may, and usually does, work for a real estate broker (firm) as a salesperson.

A **sole proprietor** is an individual broker, not a corporation, who is trading under his own name and fulfilling all the duties and functions of the principal broker in the firm.

## NECESSITY FOR LICENSE

Anyone who performs or advertises the brokerage services mentioned above must hold the appropriate license or registration issued by the Real Estate Board. Licenses are issued for brokers (firms, principal brokers, associate brokers, all known as Class I licenses) or salespersons (Class II licenses). For partnerships, associations or corporations, Virginia law requires that every member or officer of the organization who *actively participates* in the brokerage business must hold a real estate *broker* license; only holding a salesperson license does not allow the individual to be a member or officer in a real estate brokerage. Each salesperson associated or affiliated with the firm must hold a salesperson license (or for those who have fulfilled the experience, educational and testing requirements, a broker license; these individuals are associate brokers). For further information concerning qualification and procedures for licensure, see Chapter 14.

Another category of real estate professional is the **rental location agent**. Formerly required to hold a salesperson license, rental location agents are now required only to *register* with the REB. Rental location agents solicit listings of rental properties from landlords and may receive a commission if they find a tenant; they also sell listings of available rental properties to prospective tenants.

## EXEMPTIONS

Not everyone who performs real estate or related activities is required to hold a Virginia real estate license. The exemptions from licensure requirements are listed Virginia Code Par. 54-734 and include the following:

1. An owner or lessor of real estate or his regular employees may sell, rent or exchange his own property. This applies not only to individuals but also to firms such as partnerships, associations or corporations. The real estate activities must be performed in the regular course of managing the property. Examples include the following:

    • An unlicensed salesperson may be hired by a builder to sell the builder's new homes but cannot sell anyone else's homes for compensation without a license.

    • An owner may employ an unlicensed property manager to manage his apartment building.

2. An individual acting as attorney-in-fact under a duly executed power of attorney may carry out the provisions of an existing contract for the sale, lease or exchange of real property. The person who authorizes the attorney-in-fact to act must be alive at the time of completion of the transaction, because a power of attorney ceases at the death of the person granting it.

3. An attorney-at-law may sell real property if such a sale is part of the performance of his duties as attorney on a particular case. He may not, however, advertise that he can sell real property for others for compensation without a real estate broker's license.

4. A person acting under court order, such as a receiver, trustee in bankruptcy or the administrator or executor of an estate, may sell or rent the real property placed under his care if such action is part of the duties imposed on him by the court.

5. A trustee acting under the direction of a legal document, such as a trust agreement, deed of trust or will, may sell or rent the real property named in the document (or other property if authorized). He may not, however, go beyond the instructions contained in the document.

6.  A corporation may manage rental housing if it owns the rental units and if the officers, directors and member in the ownership corporation and the management corporation are the same. The corporation may not manage real estate owned by others.

License requirements in Virginia do not apply to appraisers. Auctioneers are licensed as such but can sell real property as part of an auction sale. The auctioneer may be employed by the owner of the real property or by the persons functioning as noted in items 2 through 5 above. The auctioneer may not advertise that he is authorized to sell real estate but may advertise the particular property being sold at public auction.

## LAW OF AGENCY

The law of agency prescribes relationships between agent and principal. In real estate, the primary relationships between a licensee (the real estate broker) and the principal are as follows:

1.  Broker as agent of Seller
2.  Broker as agent of Buyer and
3.  Property Manager as agent of Owner.

In all three of these relationships the agent must be a licensed broker. The agency agreement must be in writing and signed by both agent and principal. The employment contract between broker and seller is a listing agreement; that between broker and buyer is a buyer agency agreement (finder's agreement or buyer listing agreement); and that between property manager and property owner is a property management agreement. In all three cases the agent is bound by duties as a fiduciary of the principal. Normally the broker in a listing agreement or buyer agency agreement is a special agent, with specific and limited powers, while the property manager is usually a general agent, with authority to enter into certain contracts for (on behalf of) the owner.

## BEHAVIOR PERMITTED TO LICENSEES

Virginia law, as set forth in the Real Estate Board regulations, is quite explicit concerning acts permitted and prohibited to licensees. Specific provisions that apply to the brokerage business appear as Regulations #3.5.2-18, 32, 33, and 3.8 and are summarized below.

A licensee may not pay commission or other valuable consideration to a nonlicensee for performing real estate functions. Thus, a salesperson who gives prizes or money to friends or acquaintances for leads or prospects is liable to be disciplined by the REB.

The licensee may not accept payment of money or other valuable consideration for any real estate actions he performs from anyone other than his principal broker at the time of the transaction. If the seller feels that the licensee has performed very well and is deserving of extra compensation, the licensee may not accept such compensation directly; rather, the seller must pay the broker, who will then compensate the licensee. A salesperson may not receive payment for a cobrokered sale from the other broker involved, only from his own principle broker.

A licensee (salesperson or associate broker) may not represent any broker other than his principal broker without the principal broker's written consent. In areas where a multiple listing service (MLS) is operating, the MLS agreement entered into by the broker ordinarily gives consent to salespeople affiliated with each broker to show properties listed by other member brokers. In addition, individuals with broker licenses (associate brokers) may work for more than one principal broker, provided that each principal broker has signified written consent by filing a concurrent license form with the REB; this provision does not apply *in a practical way* to supervising brokers, who must be full-time, on-premises brokers supervising the operation of a branch office for one principal broker.

The licensee may not act for more than one party to a transaction without the informed consent, in writing, of all parties for whom he acts. Failure to obtain such consent may result in undisclosed dual agency and could lead to forfeiture of the agent's commission as well as disciplinary action by the REB. Such a dual agency may arise inadvertently, as when a salesperson representing a buyer shows the buyer a property listed by another associate of the same firm. In reality, both salespeople, as general agents of the same broker, *must* represent the seller under a valid listing agreement, and the salesperson working with the buyer must disclose to the buyer the broker's fiduciary obligation to the seller. This disclosure must be in writing.

A licensee may not act as agent for any principal in a real estate transaction outside his brokerage firm or sole proprietorship. For example, a person asked a licensee to help him in a real estate transaction without involving his broker ("I know and trust you, George, but I don't want the brokerage firm in on this; I just want *you* to help me"). George could not participate in any transaction as anyone's agent except under the direct supervision of his principal broker and in the name of the firm.

It may seem elementary that a licensee may not offer real property for sale or rent without the owner's knowledge and consent. Nonetheless, a real estate broker or agent has no implied authority to fix the terms of sale or to sign a contract of sale on behalf of his principal. In addition, broader issues also arise here: (1) *all* owners whose interest is being conveyed must sign all documents involved and (2) once the documents are signed, the licensee as agent has no authority to modify the terms and conditions of the agreement in any way without the knowledge and consent of all owners.

A broker's obligation to a principal is broader than the duty to follow instructions. The general rule is well settled in Virginia that a real estate broker occupies a fiduciary relationship to the principal. So long as that relation continues, the broker is under legal obligation, as well as high moral duty, to give the principal loyal service. He is bound to disclose to the principal all facts within his knowledge that are (or may be) material to the matter in which he is employed or that might influence the principal's actions. If the broker fails to meet this standard of duty, he forfeits the right to recover a commission. A broker's duty does include the obligation to solicit offers for the property listed for sale; however, the broker may not do so by representing that the owner will accept a lower price or different terms from those on the signed listing agreement.

The following scenario is, unfortunately, all too common:

Salesman A:  I'm Jim Cox, Ace Realty, calling for Jack Spot.

Salesman B:  Speaking.

A.  Jack, is your listing on Oak Street still available and is the information in the MLS book still correct?

B.  Yes, it is, but I'm sure an offer in the mid-60s would sell the property.

A.  Is it still listed at $76,500?

B.  Right.  But the seller is getting pretty desperate.

A.  Has he authorized a price reduction?

B.  No, but if he knows what's good for him, he'll take the first decent offer that comes in.

In this situation Salesman A, bringing the potential buyer, is apparently seeking properties in the $76,000 range.  Salesman B immediately offers (in effect) a $10,000 or more price reduction.  He is not authorized to reveal his seller's money situation or his seller's position with regard to urgency or anything else that might adversely affect the seller's bargaining power.

 When an offer is received, the broker's duty to communicate the offer promptly to the seller is absolute and does not depend upon whether or not the broker views the offer as a good one.

A licensee may not place a sign on any property without the owner's consent; this includes public as well as private property.  He must be aware of local ordinances concerning signs and should obtain approval from local authorities before placing open house signs on street medians or corners.  Private property rights should also be respected, and licensees should ask permission before placing directional or other signs on anyone's land.

The firm's name in a size equal to or greater than of the salesperson must be included in all advertising of any real property for sale or rent.  The listed property may never be advertised in the salesperson's own name alone, which might convey the false impression that he was a real estate *broker*.  Further, the advertisement may not in any way lend the impression that the property is for sale or rent *by owner*.

Virginia law requires the agent to disclose all pertinent information available to him about a property.  This has been interpreted to include any information on which a buyer might reasonably base a decision to purchase.  Formerly, the regulation specified disclosure of the real estate's

> . . . character, condition, location, acreage, boundaries, loan charges, loan discount, highway location or relocation, zoning restrictions, proposed zoning changes, the existence and availability of public utilities and sewer connections, taxes, and approximate closing costs. (3.5.14, 1984 REGULATIONS)

As of July 15, 1987, the language of this section was simplified to read "Failing to disclose in a timely manner to a prospective purchaser/lessee, or seller/lessor, any material information related to the property reasonably available to the licensee or registrant"; this simplification of language broadens its effect and increases the responsibility of the licensee. The specific nature of the earlier language prevented comprehensive coverage of all situations that might be encountered, but the new language makes it clear that *any* material fact is to be disclosed. In short, the licensee has a duty, not only to disclose all material facts that are known, but also to determine and disclose those facts that he should have known.

Virginia cases relevant to this disclosure rule include the following: (1) a broker was sued for telling a buyer that the property adjacent to the back of the lot he was buying was zoned residential, when in fact it was commercial and was so developed; (2) a seller in a sales contract failed to disclose to the buyer that flooding had damaged the property prior to closing, and the court awarded damages to the buyer; (3) a buyer did *not* recover damages in a case in which he moved into the property and discovered damaged bathroom floors, missing storm windows and gutters that did not work properly. In this case the seller's statement that the gutters were new was true, the missing storm windows were an open and obvious defect, and a thorough inspection (which the seller did nothing to discourage) would have shown the bathroom damage. Thus, while adequate disclosure is mandatory, the doctrine of *caveat emptor* still has enough currency to warrant caution on the part of the buyer.

The licensee must present to the seller every written offer on the property as promptly as possible and may not wait to see if better offers come in. Further, he must be sure that all parties to a transaction receive copies of all documents related to the transaction as well as written notice of any material changes to the transaction; all such copies and notices should be distributed in a timely manner, so that no opportunities or advantages would be lost due to delay.

Brokers and salespeople may not make any misrepresentation or false promises in order to induce sellers or buyers to purchase. A false promise would be, "Mr. Seller, I will sell your property within a month." While the salesperson may guarantee that he will market the property to the full extent of his ability, he cannot guarantee the behavior of the marketplace or that it will produce a ready, willing and able buyer within a certain time.

The rules for disclosure of interest are explicit and firm. A licensee may not acquire any interest in real property for his family, or any member of it or any entity of which he is part owner, without disclosing this to the seller *in writing*. If the licensee is selling real property in which he or she has any of the interests referred to above, that fact must be revealed in writing to any prospective purchaser as well. Examples of possible wordings for such disclosures may include:

- Buyer is real estate licensee in Virginia.
- Seller is a licensed real estate salesperson (broker).
- Listing salesperson is daughter of the seller.

These or similar wordings in listing contracts and in sales contracts will serve notice to all interested parties of the status of the licensee. (In newspaper advertisements or other brief notices, the words "owner/agent" may serve as notice.)

The Real Estate Board may take disciplinary action against anyone violating the regulations cited above; for licensees this is true whether the improprieties occurred in the licensee's personal or professional capacity.

## PLACE OF BUSINESS

The Virginia Real Estate Board regulations define place of business as an office where

> . . . the principal broker, either through his own efforts or through the efforts of his employees or associates, regularly transacts the business of a real estate broker...And [where] the principal broker and his employees or associates can receive business calls and direct business calls to be made. (3.1A)

The place of business can be in a residence provided the office is separate from the living quarters and is accessible to the public, and such necessary facilities as bathrooms and parking facilities are available. Any such place of business must comply with zoning requirements and any applicable deed restrictions. The REB or its agents may inspect any place of business to verify compliance with the law.

Each place of business must be identified by a sign stating that it is a real estate brokerage (subject to local sign ordinances). Within each main place of business (main office, corporate headquarters, etc.) the broker must display his Virginia real estate license and those of his licensees. The licenses must be displayed together, so that the public can readily determine the names of the licensees. The individual licensee is issued a pocket card identifying him as a licensee of the Real Estate Board.

Whenever the brokerage changes business name or location, the REB must be notified in writing of the change. The notice must be accompanied by the licenses of all licensees associated with the firm. The Board must receive the notice within ten days of the change and will reissue licenses with the new name or location for the unexpired term.

Individual licensees must keep the REB informed of their current home addresses. If the licensee's tenure with his broker is terminated for any reason, voluntary or not, the principal broker must notify the board and the licensee of the termination. The broker must return the licensee's license to the board by certified mail within ten days of the date of termination, as noted on the license and must also sign the license. If a salesperson terminates tenure with a broker, his active listings remain the property of the broker; however, depending upon the circumstances of termination, the salesperson may still collect commissions on sales, negotiated but not yet closed, prior to termination.

Each place of business, including branch offices, must be managed by an on-premises real estate broker, who supervises only that office and who is expected to be at the office or within easy access during regular business hours. One branch office license is issued by the board for each branch office maintained in Virginia. However, only the branch office license appears at the particular branch office; all licensees' licenses are displayed at the main place of business.

For information concerning licensing requirements, see Chapter 14; for information concerning escrow deposits and brokers' management of funds, see Chapter 11.

## QUESTIONS

1.   Which of the following must be licensed in order to practice his or her occupation in Virginia?

     a.   Real estate salesperson or broker
     b.   Rental location agent
     c.   Appraiser
     d.   Mortgage lender

2.   Which of the following combinations may legally form a real estate brokerage partnership?

     a.   Two licensed real estate brokers
     b.   Two licensed real estate salespeople
     c.   One licensed salesperson and one licensed broker
     d.   A real estate broker and an unlicensed appraiser

3.   Any individual holding a broker license in Virginia who is not a principal broker is, according to REB regulations, a(n):

     a.   affiliate broker.
     b.   supervising broker.
     c.   managing broker.
     d.   associate broker.

4.   A salesperson's relation to his broker is that of a:

     a.   dual agent.
     b.   universal agent.
     c.   special agent.
     d.   general agent.

5.   Which of the following persons would be required to hold a Virginia real estate license?

     a.   An appraiser appraising real estate
     b.   Your neighbor, for renting out your property for $40 a month
     c.   A mortgage banker, selling property at foreclosure
     d.   The executor of an estate, selling the decedent's home

6. Which of the following would be exempt from the licensure requirement in real estate in Virginia?

   a. A homeowner selling his own residence
   b. A tradesman who receives $100 every time a lead he gives to a licensee results in a closing
   c. An attorney-at-law advertising that she can sell homes
   d. An auctioneer advertising that he can sell homes

7. How does the death of the principal affect the authority of the attorney-in-fact?

   a. The authority continues unaffected.
   b. The authority ceases at the principal's death.
   c. The heirs must honor any contracts entered by the principal, and the attorney-in-fact remains in authority.
   d. Any documents needed to complete transactions entered by the principal should be back-dated to before his death.

8. Where may a licensee place an open house sign without obtaining the permission of the owner on whose property the sign is placed?

   a. In the median of a public street or highway
   b. On the city-owned portion of corner lots
   c. On vacant land
   d. None of the above

9. Which of the following advertisements would comply with Virginia law?

   a. A salesperson who is also a builder advertises his new homes using only his name.
   b. A salesperson lists his own property with his company, then advertises using only his home telephone number.
   c. A salesperson advertises an open house, giving his own name under the broker's name.
   d. A salesperson/builder advertises the homes he has built as "for sale by owner."

10. Salesperson Glenda "forgets" to tell a buyer about a defect in the house; later, upon being sued by the buyer, she defends herself by saying that she was working for the seller, and that the buyer was responsible for finding defects. Is the salesperson right?

    a. She is correct in every detail.
    b. No; she was working for the buyer and should have disclosed the defect.
    c. No; even though she worked for the seller, she owed the buyer (who relied on her word) full disclosure concerning the property.
    d. No; she should have explained the doctrine of *caveat emptor* to the buyer, who would then have obtained a property inspection.

## ANSWERS

1.   a.   Real estate salespeople and brokers must be licensed; rental location agents must be registered; and appraisers and mortgage lenders are not licensed.

2.   a.

3.   d.   An associate broker is anyone with the broker license other than a principal broker. A supervising broker is an associate broker placed in charge of a branch office (sometimes referred to as a managing broker).

4.   d.   The salesperson signs listings and sales contracts on behalf of the broker (subject, however, to broker's supervision). The broker, however, is a special agent to the principal.

5.   b.   One such act constitutes practicing as a real estate broker, which requires a license. The other answers are all examples of exemptions from necessity for license.

6.   a.   Anyone can sell his own home. The other answers cite instances where a license would be required for practice in real estate.

7.   b.

8.   d.

9.   c.   In answers a and d, adequate disclosure of licensee status is lacking; in b the broker lacks sufficient identification.

10.   c.

# 6

# Listing Agreements

The standard types of listings--open, exclusive-agency and exclusive-right-to-sell--are all legal in Virginia, as is the multiple listing. Virginia law, however, specifically prohibits a "net" listing in which a net amount to the seller is specified, with the broker receiving as commission any amount in excess of the seller's net. Virginia law also specifies that exclusive-agency or exclusive-right-to-sell listings must have a definite termination date. The owner must be furnished a copy of the listing at the time it is signed.

While "signature pending" listings are permitted in some parts of Virginia on a temporary basis, valid listings must contain the signatures of all owners of the property.

## LISTING FORMS

The Real Estate Board does not establish standard listing forms; consequently, a wide variety of forms are to be found throughout the state. Reproduced on the following pages is a representative listing form from the Massanutten Board of Realtors. Since listing forms change frequently and vary widely from one market area to another, licensees should be thoroughly familiar with current local forms in any area in which they wish to transact business.

In any listing form, the blanks should be filled in; they are rarely optional or discretionary. If an item does not apply, the notation "N/A" should be used. Finding accurate information for each item may require time-consuming and occasionally difficult research; nonetheless, it is necessary.

It is legal in Virginia for land to be owned by a land trust, so that only the name of the trust or trustee would appear, rather than the name of the trustor or beneficiary. It is also legal for the owner's name to appear only on that portion of the listing held by the broker, so that the owner's name does not appear in the multiple listing service book. However, it is illegal to sell real property without the owner's written consent; consequently, verbal (oral) agreements for builders or others to sell land for which the true owner (whose name does not appear on the listing) is to be paid at closing should not be permitted.

Some items on the listing forms may have to be entered as approximations, such as mortgage balance (until a payoff statement is available from the lender) or age of the dwelling; naturally, accurate figures should be used wherever possible.

Changes in property status must be communicated to the broker and to the MLS as soon as possible after they occur; any changes involving financial responsibility on the seller's part (such as a change in price or discount points) must normally be authorized in writing by the seller.

## SAMPLE LISTING FORM

The top portion of the listing form is submitted for inclusion in the local MLS book, so that all brokers within the MLS may have access to information concerning the property. In general, the information concerns physical aspects of the property (size, construction, rooms), legal and financial aspects (description, terms, taxes), and which personal property items convey with the property; the listing broker and salesperson are also specified.

The bottom portion of the listing is the actual agreement between seller and broker. The date of the agreement (line 1) is often, but not necessarily, the same date as the effective date of the listing (line 7, beginning). The first paragraph names the parties and time limit of the agreement, together with the duties of the broker (Realtor) and the owner. The commission rate or fee is specified in line 11. The "Exclusive Authorization to Sell" that heads the agreement is further explicated in lines 13-15, which also include the protective clause (extension clause). Placement of a sign on the property is expressly authorized in line 19.

Lines 21-23 are important in establishing the responsibility of the seller for representations made in the listing and to purchasers. Lines 24 and 25 specify compliance with fair housing statutes.

In lines 26-28, the owner warrants that he will convey the property by general warranty deed, free of encumbrances but subject to applicable restrictive covenants.

Lines 29-32 state that the listing will be submitted to the Board of Realtors and the multiple listing service; however, lines 38 and 39 permit the owner to refuse to have the listing included in the MLS.

**Figure 6.1**: Sample Exclusive Authorization to Sell

| Address & Area | | | | Rms | Bdrms | Baths | $ | |
|---|---|---|---|---|---|---|---|---|
| Legal | | | | | Directions: | | | |
| Const/Style | | Age | | Roof | | | | |
| Terms | | Lot Size | | Zoning | | | | |
| Fin.Sq.Ft.Bsmt | 1st | 2nd | Ext.Dim. | | Rooms | Size 1st Floor | Size 2nd Floor | |
| Taxes | I | Bsmt. | | | Foyer | | | |
| Mineral Rights | | Fireplace | Siding | | Living | | | |
| Sign | Possession | Walls | | | Family | | | |
| Pub.School | | Floors | | | Dining | | | |
| | | Cabinets | | | Kitchen | | | |
| Water | | Rge-Ovn. | Refrig. | | Br'fast | | | |
| Sewer | | Dishw. | Disp. | | Bedrm | | | |
| Elect.Co. | Amps. | Wtr.Htr. | Air Cond. | | Bedrm | | | |
| Heat | Yr./Mo. | Attic | | | Bedrm | | | |
| Insulation | | | SW | SD | | | | |
| | | | | | Baths | | | |
| | | | | | Utility | | | |
| | | | | | Garage | Outblds. | | |
| Data Not Warranted By Broker | | | | | Show | | | |
| Salesman & Phone | | | Owner | | | | | |
| Firm & Phone | | | | Co-op % | | MLS # | | |

MASSANUTTEN BOARD OF REALTORS MULTIPLE LISTING SERVICE
EXCLUSIVE AUTHORIZATION TO SELL
(This is a legally binding contract. If not understood, seek competent advice.)

Date: _____   1

In consideration of the services of_____ (herein called "Realtor") to be rendered   2
to the undersigned (herein called "Owner"), and of the promise of Realtor to make reasonable efforts to obtain a purchaser therefor,   3

Owner hereby lists with Realtor the real estate and all improvements thereon which are described as _____   4
_____   5
(herein called the "property"), and Owner hereby grants to Realtor the exclusive and irrevocable right to sell such property from 12:00   6

Noon on _____, 19___until Midnight on _____, 19___ (herein called "period of time"), for the price   7
of _____ Dollars ($_____) or for such lower prices and upon such   8
other terms (including exchange) as Owner may subsequently authorize during the period of time. It is expressly understood that this   9
agreement in no way constitutes a contractual obligation between the Multiple Listing Service and the Owner.   10

It is understood by Owner that the above sum or any other prices subsequently authorized by Owner shall include a cash fee of _____   11
per cent of such price or lower prices, which shall be payable by Owner to Realtor upon execution by any Purchaser or Purchasers of a   12
contract of sale of the property during the period of time and whether or not Realtor was a procuring cause of any such contract of sale.   13

Such compensation shall be paid if the property is sold, conveyed, or otherwise transferred within_____days after the termination of this   14
agreement or any extension thereof to anyone with whom the agent has negotiated prior to final termination, provided the Owner has re-   15
ceived notice in writing including the name of prospective purchasers, before or upon termination of this agreement or any extension   16
thereof. However, the Owner shall not be obligated to pay such compensation if a valid listing agreement is entered into during the   17
term of said protection period with another licensed real estate broker and the sale, lease, or exchange of the property is made during   18
the term of said protection period. Realtor is hereby authorized by Owner to place a "For Sale" sign on the property and to remove all   19
signs of other brokers or salesmen during the period of time, and Owner hereby agrees to make the property available to Realtor at all   20
reasonable hours for the purpose of showing it to prospective Purchasers. It is expressly understood that the property data herein listed   21
are representations of the Owner and are correct to the best of the Owner's knowledge. The Owner hereby authorizes the Realtor to   22
quote those Owner representations to prospective Purchasers. The Realtor is not responsible for vandalism, theft, or damage of any na-   23
ture whatsoever to the property except any damage caused by the Realtor. Owner agrees that the property is to be listed, offered for   24
sale, and sold without respect to the race, color, religion, or national origin of any Purchaser or Purchasers.   25

If a sale of the property is consummated during the period of time or within_____ days thereafter, Owner agrees to convey the property   26
to the Purchaser by general warranty deed with the usual English Covenants of title and free and clear from all encumbrances, tenancies,   27
liens (for taxes or otherwise), but subject to applicable restrictive covenants of record.   28

It is expressly understood and agreed that the below named Realtor, upon execution of this contract, will submit this listing to the Massa-   29
nutten Board of Realtors Multiple Listing Service for distribution to all its members, and that any and all members of the Massanutten   30
Board of Realtors Multiple Listing Service shall have the right to show and sell this property in accordance with the terms contained herein   31
unless otherwise provided below.   32

Witness to signature(s) and seal(s):    Owner _____   33
Date Signed: _____    Owner _____   34
Firm & Phone _____    Owner _____   35
Address _____    Address _____   36
Agent & Phone _____    City/State/Phone _____   37
The advantages and benefits of the Multiple Listing Service have been explained to me and by signing this statement I hereby acknowl-   38
edge that I do not desire to have my property submitted to the Massanutten Board of Realtors Multiple Listing Service.   39

(Seal) _____    _____(Seal)   40
(Owner)                                             (Owner)   41

## QUESTIONS

1.  Which of the following is required by law for an exclusive-right-to-sell listing in Virginia?

    a.  Owner's name must appear in information block (MLS)
    b.  Definite termination date
    c.  Extension or protective clause
    d.  Precise acreage

2.  Which type of listing is prohibited in Virginia?

    a.  Net listing
    b.  Exclusive-agency listing
    c.  General listing
    d.  Open listing

3.  At the time of taking a listing, which of the following is the most important thing the listing salesperson must do?

    a.  Place a sign on the property.
    b.  Advertise the property in a local newspaper.
    c.  Furnish a copy of the signed listing form to the seller.
    d.  Arrange to hold an open house as soon as possible.

4.  In which of the following cases could the true owner's name *not* appear on the listing agreement?

    a.  Builder is selling for owner and will pay the owner at settlement.
    b.  A land trust is holding property for an unnamed beneficiary.
    c.  Someone who wishes his/her identity kept secret signs an assumed name.
    d.  None of the above

5.  Which of the following changes to a listing (as shown in an MLS book) would require the seller's signature?

    a.  Listed sales price
    b.  Discount points authorized to be paid by seller
    c.  Seller to pay part of all of buyer's closing cost
    d.  All of the above

## ANSWERS

1.  b.  The termination date is required by REB regulations. The owner's name may be withheld from the MLS information block. The extension or protective clause is included in most exclusive-right-to-sell listings to protect the broker but is not required. Precise acreage is not required if land is being sold in gross.

2.  a.  The net listing is specifically prohibited. Note that "general listing" is a synonym for "open listing."

3.  c.  The REB regulations require that the seller be given a copy of the signed listing at the time it is secured. The other answers may all be advisable, but none is required by law.

4.  b.  It must be understood, however, that in one sense the land trust *is* the true owner; it merely owns the property on behalf of someone else. The beneficiary, however, has in many respects a stronger ownership than the land trust. Answer a is illegal, since the true owner has not signed. Answer c violates laws requiring an identifiable grantor having a legal existence, unless the assumed name is recorded so as to show the person's actual identity.

5.  d.  All the choices show financial responsibility on the seller's part; he or she must, therefore, verify and sign the changes in writing.

# 7

## Interests in Real Estate

The interests in real estate dealt with in *Modern Real Estate Practice* are found, with some variations, in Virginia; this chapter deals with the state's applications of governmental powers, life estates, dower/curtesy, easements and riparian rights.

### GOVERNMENT POWERS

#### Eminent Domain

In Virginia, the power of eminent domain is provided by the state constitution and is covered in great detail by statutes.

Virginia law generally parallels the provisions dealt with in the main text, but provides that easements, ingress and egress rights, flowage rights and similar rights and uses all constitute "property" for which just compensation must be paid if they are taken *or damaged* by the Commonwealth by eminent domain. In a condemnation suit, the compensation is divided among all those with an interest in the property. Generally, "just compensation" means the fair market value of the property at the time of the taking. Payment of just compensation is a prerequisite to passing of title to the property. Further, a genuine (but ineffectual) effort must have been made to purchase the property before beginning condemnation proceedings.

If the parties do not agree upon the compensation for the land, commissioners are appointed to hold a hearing and issue a report determining the amount. Virginia's Condemnation Act provides for a two-stage proceeding. First, the court determines the fair market value of the land taken and the damage (if any) to the remaining land. Second, if payment occurs, the court determines the rights and claims of all persons entitled to compensation.

The real estate licensee must disclose to all interested parties that a parcel or an entire area is planned for condemnation. For example, a seller indicates that a governmental authority has made an offer to acquire the property because condemnation proceedings are contemplated. Any prospective buyer should be made aware of this information. Obviously, condemnation can affect the value of property; for example, if property is condemned for street construction, the value of adjacent parcels may increase due to the access provided by the street.

#### Escheat

When a person dies with neither will nor heirs but owns real property in Virginia, the title to the property passes or "escheats" to the Commonwealth. If someone has possession of escheated land by lease for a term of years or has rights to rent or other profit from the property, he may continue to hold the lease, rent or profit. Creditors of the decedent whose land escheats to the Commonwealth may file claims for recovery even after the land has escheated.


## ESTATES IN LAND


### Fee Simple

Fee simple is a freehold estate of inheritance, free of conditions and of indefinite duration, with unrestricted right to transfer the property. It is impossible for one party to own a fee simple title while another simultaneously holds a life estate in the property. Unless otherwise stated, a deed is construed to pass an estate in fee simple. In Virginia the term *estate* usually implicitly includes rights of dower and curtesy.

Although an attorney must review all closing documents, including the deed, the prudent real estate professional may also review the deed to verify that it clearly transfers an interest in fee simple, if such was called for in the sales contract.

Virginia requires freehold estates to be created in writing by deed or will. Upon the death of the owner of a fee simple estate, it passes as provided in the will or (if there is no will) to the heirs as specified in the descent statutes.


### Fee Simple Defeasible

In Virginia the wording that creates a defeasible fee or fee simple determinable is "until" or "as long as" or "while" or "during."


### Life Estates

The Virginia statutes conform to the definitions in the main text; however, the following notes may be helpful.

Generally, a life tenant cannot make a valid lease for a period extended beyond the term of the life tenancy; the lessee's rights would be ended, since the remainderman would have immediate right to possession. A life interest may be sold in Virginia; the state maintains an actuarial table specifying what percentage of the fair market value the property may bring to the life tenant, depending upon age (the table supplies values for ages up to 105 years).

The real estate professional may seldom encounter a life estate in practice. However, he should be aware that in order to transfer any property being sold and occupied by a life tenant it is necessary to obtain signatures of *both* the life tenant and any party with a future interest in the property. In Virginia, a life tenant must pay all real estate taxes on the property.

## Remainder, Reversion and Possibility of Reverter

There are estates in *possession* and estates in *expectancy*. Thus, a person such as a reversioner or remainderman may have title to property and yet not have the right of present possession or enjoyment of the property.

Since a life estate is essentially an interruption in a succession of fee simple estates, a **remainder estate** is defined as what is left of a grant in fee after a preceding part of the same grant has been possessed as a life estate. The reminder and the life estate are created at the same time and by the same instrument, and the remainder interest arises immediately on thetermination of the life estate. It is the duty of the remainderman or owner of the expected fee to *wait*, since he has no present right in the property. Remainders may be vested (e.g., life estate to son, remainder interest to his children) or contingent (e.g., property to pass to remainderman if he survives the life tenant).

A **reversion** is the residue of an estate left to the grantor or his heirs, whose right of possession only begins at the termination of a life estate. This should be distinguished from a *possibility of reverter,* which arises from a defeasible fee that may last forever or may terminate if a condition of the grant is violated. In the latter case, no estate of ownership is presently indicated; there is only the possibility of having the fee at some future date.

## DOWER AND CURTESY

Virginia is one of the few states that have not abolished the common law concepts of dower and curtesy. Curtesy rights have been made identical to dower rights. Dower and curtesy have been converted from life estates to *estates in fee simple* in Virginia. The requisites of dower or curtesy are as follows:

1. The parties must be married.
2. One spouse must own the property.
3. The property must be held as an inheritable estate.
4. The owning spouse must die first.
5. The estate must continue as a fee simple.

By statute in Virginia the requirement for curtesy that children be born alive during the marriage has been abolished. During the life of the husband, the wife has a mere contingent right of dower, which may be conveyed or relinquished. A widow's dower in land is subject to a mortgage, judgment or other encumbrance on the property. Should the husband convey, mortgage or contract to convey land to another, the wife's contingent right of dower remains; should she survive her husband, she may enforce her right against the grantee, mortgagee or vendee, since her claim is superior.

It is critical, where the property to be conveyed is owned by husband and wife, that the deed conveying the property be signed by both spouses. Although this may seem elementary, there are instances where this has not been accomplished and litigation has arisen. Further, the prudent real estate professional should take whatever steps are necessary to insure that each spouse actually executes the deed before a notary to avoid any possibility of forgery.

Moreover, the real estate professional should satisfy himself that the signing spouse is *competent*, thus avoiding a claim to the contrary by a dissatisfied relative. In Virginia, a final divorce decree terminates the widow's contingent dower interest. In some cases, it may be proper to request proof of the divorce to guard against an abandoned spouse contesting the transfer.

Virginia law now permits a spouse's *grantor* to defeat the other spouse's dower or curtesy right by creating a sole and separate estate. A surviving spouse is not entitled to dower or curtesy in the equitable separate estate of the deceased spouse if that right to the property was *expressly excluded* by the instrument creating the interest, or if the instrument described the estate as his or her sole and separate equitable estate. For the husband, this individual ownership is characterized as *homme sole*; for the wife it is *femme sole*.

## HOMESTEAD EXEMPTION

In Virginia only a householder or head of a family may have the benefit of a homestead exemption. A husband and wife, living together, may both be deemed householders if each contributes to the maintenance of the household. The householder is entitled to hold exempt from unsecured debts any real or personal property, the value of which cannot exceed $5,000. The exemption would not apply against claims for the purchase price of the homestead property, mechanics' liens and claims for taxes, among others. The householder's claim to homestead must be made either by deed or by an inventory under oath, depending on whether the homestead is in real or personal property. The owner of the homestead may sell or encumber it.

A deed of trust held as a lien against a homestead has priority over the homestead exemption; the property may be sold at foreclosure to satisfy the debt.

In addition to the estate (not exceeding $5,000 in value), the householder is entitled to hold exempt, among others, these items: the family Bible, wedding and engagement rings and a burial plot.

As a practical matter, the real estate agent may be unaware that a homestead deed has been filed; such information is usually revealed in the title search by an attorney or title examiner. If a homestead deed does come to the agent's attention, he should be aware that the homeowner's filing of the deed could indicate financial difficulties or even pending bankruptcy (contemplated or filed) or that judgments may be of record; in any event, further investigation is warranted before transferring the property.

## EASEMENTS

Easements (the right of one person to use the land of another for a specific purpose) are frequently revealed during a title search in preparing for a closing. Easements for water and sewer mains, telephone lines, power lines and the like are normal and necessary and (beyond disclosure to the purchaser) should not concern the real estate professional. However, other easements, particularly those not readily apparent by viewing the property, require disclosure and examination of a survey.

## Easements Appurtenant and in Gross

Virginia law parallels the treatment in the main text; the following amplifications may be of interest.

A personal easement in gross cannot be transferred by the individual to whom it was given, nor can it pass by inheritance. A distinguishing feature of the two types is that the easement appurtenant has a dominant tenement and an easement in gross does not.

## Creating an Easement

As shown in *Modern Real Estate Practice,* an easement may be acquired by express grant or may be created by covenant or agreement. However, in Virginia the owner of a dominant tenement may convey the land *without* the easement: where the easement is not by necessity and the appurtenance is *expressly excluded* by the grant, it will not convey. If a grantor conveys land by deed and describes it as bounded by a road or street that the grantor owns, he implies that the right-of-way exists and that the grantee acquires the benefit of it.

In Virginia, if the width of a right-of-way is not specified in the grant, it is limited to the width as it existed at the time of the grant. If an easement has a definite location, it may be changed with the express or implied consent of the interested parties (it could be implied from the acts of the parties).

An easement reserved by the grantor in the property conveyed must be expressly stated.

## Easement by Necessity

An easement by necessity arises from an implied grant or reservation. When a grantor conveys property, he conveys whatever is necessary for its beneficial use and retains whatever is necessary for the beneficial use of the land he still owns. In Virginia, to establish a right-of-way by necessity, the dominant and servient tracts *must have belonged to the same person* at some past time.

Where a parcel of land is conveyed that is surrounded by the grantor's retained land (or by lands of others as well as the grantor's land) and no means of access is expressly provided, the law implies an easement in favor of the grantee *over the retained land of the grantor.* The rule of strict necessity is not limited to absolute necessity but to a reasonable necessity, as distinguished from mere convenience. An easement by necessity does not arise if there is already another mode of access to the land, even if it is less convenient or more expensive to develop.

## Easement by Prescription

In Virginia, to establish an easement by prescription, the court must find that the use was (1) adverse, (2) under a claim of right, (3) exclusive, (4) continuous, (5) uninterrupted and (6) with the knowledge and acquiescence of the landowner for at least 20 years. "Tacking" or combining successive periods of continuous uninterrupted use by different parties is permitted in Virginia. An easement by prescription will not arise from permission by the owner of the servient estate; the use once granted by permission is presumed to continue likewise unless the user's conduct is sufficient to alert the servient tenant that the user is now asserting a claim adverse and hostile to his rights. To ripen into a prescriptive right, the claim to use must then meet all of the requirements enumerated above, including time.

## Terminating Easements

While the possible ways to end an easement mentioned in the main text also exist in Virginia, it should be noted that an easement may be extinguished if the servient estate is conveyed to a purchaser without notice of the easement. It is not necessary that a document terminate the easement in the clerk's office for the county where the land is located.

## RIPARIAN RIGHTS

Riparian rights pertain to land abutting a waterway. Under Virginia law, riparian rights constitute "property" and are severable from the land to which they were once appurtenant (i.e., a former owner can retain or a current owner can convey such rights). A riparian right is not an easement to pass over the water, nor a privilege to use the surface; rather, it is a *property right* to the soil under the water. All riparian owners along a stream have the same right to the use and enjoyment of its waters, qualified by the right of the others to have the waterway substantially preserved in size, flow and purity. Injury to an owner's riparian rights entitles him to damages.

A riparian property owner has no right to divert a stream from its usual course to the injury of other persons. In Virginia, by statute, a riparian owner on *navigable* waters owns the land within his boundaries to the low water mark. If this mark changes, either to the advantage or disadvantage of the riparian owner, it remains the true boundary. Title to land between the low water mark and the line of navigability of public waters in Virginia belongs to the Commonwealth, but the riparian owner has a qualified right in the same land.

The rights of a riparian owner on a navigable river are

1. the right to enjoy the natural advantages conferred upon the land by its adjacency to the water;

2. the right of access to water, including right-of-way to and from navigable parts;

3. the right to build a pier or wharf out to the navigable water, subject to state regulations;

4. the right to accretions or alluvium; and

5. the right to make reasonable use of the water as it flows past the land.

## QUESTIONS

1.  Which of the following could not be taken by condemnation in Virginia?

    a.  A county taking a farmer's cropland for a highway
    b.  The state taking from a private woodland for a roadside visitor center
    c.  City of Charlottesville taking from the University of Virginia for public parking
    d.  Port Authority of Hampton Roads taking riparian rights for a pier


2.  "Just compensation" for condemnation purposes means:

    a.  fair market value at the time of the taking.
    b.  fair market value at the time of purchase by the current owner.
    c.  fair market value less court costs and attorneys' fees.
    d.  a statutory percentage of fair market value.


3.  Which of the following conditions is necessary for condemnation to proceed?

    a.  The owner must consent.
    b.  A genuine but ineffective effort to purchase must be made.
    c.  The owner must have a property appraisal.
    d.  A statement of alternative solutions to the taking must be supplied to the owner by the condemning authority.


4.  Which of the following items of information (if true) must the licensee disclose to a prospective purchaser?

    a.  The land to be bought has been condemned by the city.
    b.  A neighboring parcel is on notice that condemnation proceedings will soon begin.
    c.  The city planning commission is holding hearings concerning a parcel a block away.
    d.  All of the above


5.  Smith rents property from Brown, who dies during the lease but has neither will nor heirs.  As a result of this situation:

    a.  Smith inherits the land from Brown.
    b.  the land escheats to the state, but Smith remains a tenant.
    c.  the land escheats, but Smith's lease is terminated.
    d.  the land cannot escheat until the end of the lease.

6.    Bragg, a homeowner, dies with no will and no heirs.  Before death he had repairs done on the house by Willett, but no payment was made.  What is the situation now?

a.    As a creditor, Willett may still file a claim for recovery.
b.    Since the land has escheated to the state and no one may claim against the state, Willett is out of luck.
c.    As the primary creditor for the deceased, Willett may claim the land.
d.    The land may not escheat until all claims, including Willett's, are paid in full.

7.    Freda owns property in fee simple.  She wishes to deed her land in such a way that she will continue as fee simple owner, while at the same time her sister Ella will be owner of a full interest as a life estate.  This situation is:

a.    joint tenancy.
b.    tenancy in sorority.
c.    a limited partnership.
d.    impossible.

8.    Brenda is the owner of a life estate in real property, with Robert as remainderman.  Brenda wishes to sell the property and lists it with Broker Klein.  Can the broker perform in this situation?

a.    No; a life estate cannot be sold in Virginia.
b.    Yes; since a deed is construed to convey land in fee simple, Broker Klein can market the property normally.
c.    Yes, but Broker Klein must obtain both Brenda's and Robert's signatures on all documents.
d.    Only if he can persuade Robert to be the buyer.

9.    Which of the following would not have to pay real estate taxes on the property?

a.    Owner of fee simple estate
b.    Owner of fee simple defeasible estate
c.    Owner of life estate
d.    None of the above

10.    When a life estate is in effect, what is the duty of the remainderman?

a.    To wait for the death of the life tenant
b.    To supervise the life tenant's ownership
c.    To pay the life tenant's life insurance and hazard insurance
d.    To administer the life tenant's estate after death

11.    What is the status of dower and curtesy rights in Virginia?

    a.    Dower and curtesy have been abolished.
    b.    Dower is a fee simple estate; curtesy is a life estate.
    c.    Dower and curtesy are identical rights in fee simple.
    d.    None of the above12.Which of the following would result in loss of dower right?

12.    Which of the following would result in loss of dower right?

    a.    Death of the owning spouse
    b.    Divorce
    c.    Owning spouse merely a tenant in common of the property
    d.    Owning spouse ruled incompetent after conveying property

13.    Which of the following statements is true concerning the homestead exemption?

    a.    Since the exemption is automatic, every homeowner has one.
    b.    The homeowner's voluntary filing for homestead may indicate financial difficulties.
    c.    The exemption is good against taxes, mechanics' liens and deeds of trust against the property.
    d.    The $5,000 exemption includes the family Bible, a wedding ring and a burial plot.

14.    Burgess's land has an appurtenant easement to cross Fahey's land; when Burgess sells to Graham, he wishes to do so without permitting the easement to continue.  Can he do so?

    a.    Yes, if the easement is expressly excluded by the grant.
    b.    Yes, if the easement is not mentioned in the grant.
    c.    No, because an appurtenant easement runs with the land.
    d.    No, it would require sale of Fahey's land as well.

15.    Which of the following is true of an easement by necessity?

    a.    It must be an appurtenant easement.
    b.    Both dominant and servient estates must at some past time have been owned by the same person.
    c.    The only reasonable means of access is over the servient estate.
    d.    All of the above

16.   Granville has a ten-foot easement through Hester's forested lot for the purpose of walking to the bank of the Otter River.  He widens the path to 14 feet to accommodate his panel truck so he can launch his boat.  Hester is furious.  **What is the situation?**

  a.   Since Granville's original use was by permission, Hester can do nothing.
  b.   The new use is hostile; if not stopped within 20 years, it could become an easement by prescription.
  c.   The additional four feet is a reasonable extension of the original easement and must simply be granted.
  d.   If Granville continues to use the extension for 15 years, the original easement becomes his by adverse possession, and the additional four feet is an easement appurtenant.

17.   Which of the following is not true of riparian rights in Virginia?

  a.   It is a property right to soil under the water.
  b.   Land on navigable waters is owned only to the low water mark and is subject to changes of that mark.
  c.   Riparian rights are appurtenant to the land and cannot be severed or separated from it.
  d.   On navigable waters, the landowner may build a pier or wharf out to the navigable waters.

18.   When may a riparian property owner divert the stream?

  a.   Never
  b.   Whenever his purpose requires him to do so
  c.   Upon agreement with the owners of adjacent property
  d.   Only if the diversion will not injure other owners

## ANSWERS

1.  c.  State universities are exempt from condemnation. The other answers are all legal condemnations.

2.  a.

3.  b.  Only if an effort to purchase was made and rejected does the condemning body have to initiate proceedings. That body will order the appraisal. No statement of alternatives is necessary.

4.  d.

5.  b.  A valid lease survives transfer of the property. Escheat technically occurs immediately at death, so that there is no gap in the chain of title.

6.  a.  Escheat does not prevent a creditor from filing claims.

7.  d.  The same property may not be held simultaneously as a fee simple estate and a life estate. Tenancy in sorority doesn't exist.

8.  c.  In order to convey a fee simple title, both the life estate and the remainder interest must be conveyed.

9.  d.

10. a.  Life tenant has full ownership during his term; his limitation is on conveying an inheritable interest in the property, which he does not have. Life tenant needs no supervision and presumably pays his own insurance. The life estate is not in effect after life tenant's death.

11. c.

12. b.

13. b.  Answer d is incorrect, because the named items are exempt in addition to the $5,000.

14. a.

15.    d.

16.    b.    The original easement granted permission, but the new use is hostile and must actually be stopped or prevented by Hester; this would terminate the original easement as well.

17.    c.    In Virginia, riparian rights can be severed from the land itself and can be conveyed; they are also subject to condemnation even if the dry land is not condemned.

18.    d.

# 8

# How Ownership Is Held

This chapter examines forms of real estate ownership recognized in Virginia. Individuals may own property as a sole and separate estate or as co-owners with others. Property ownership may be in trust. Ownership of condominiums, time-shares and cooperative interest is recognized and governed by Virginia statutes.

## CO-OWNERSHIP

### Tenancy in Common

Virginia's tenancy in common parallels the attributes discussed in the main text: there is unity of possession and a deceased tenant's interest passes to the heirs or by will. This tenancy may be created by (1) an express limitation to two or more persons to hold land as tenants in common (2) a grant of part interest in one's land to a stranger (3) a devise or grant of land to two or more persons to be divided between them and (4) a breakup of estates in joint tenancy.

A tenant in common way convey his undivided interest; however, a contract by one tenant in common relating to the whole estate is voidable by the cotenants who did not join in the contract, even though the contracting cotenant may himself be bound.

The real estate agent must remember that a deceased cotenant's interest, in passing through his will or to his heirs, is subject to the dower or curtesy rights of the surviving spouse; since there is no right to survivorship, it does not pass to a surviving cotenant.

### Joint Tenancy

Virginia's joint tenancy is similar to that described in the main text: the four unities (time, title, interest, possession) must be present. However, Virginia's interpretation of unity of interest points out that one joint tenant cannot be a tenant for life and another for years or one cannot be a tenant in fee and another for life. Joint tenancy is always created by act of the parties, never by descent or operation of law. The doctrine of survivorship was abolished in Virginia by statute; the legislature intended to place joint tenants in the same situation as tenants in common as far as dower and curtesy are concerned. If the deed expressly creates a joint tenancy *with right of survivorship* as at common law, then on the death of a joint tenant the entire estate continues in the surviving tenant or tenants. The surviving spouse of the deceased joint tenant has no dower or curtesy rights, and the deceased's creditors have no claim against the enlarged interests of the surviving tenants. A property owner who wishes to have the property pass at his death to a particular person frequently creates a joint tenancy as a substitute for a will.

A tenant in common or joint tenant who commits waste may be liable to cotenants for damages.  By statute in Virginia a joint tenant or tenant in common may demand an accounting against a cotenant for receiving more than his fair share of rents and profits from the property.  A joint tenant or tenant in common who improves the common property at his own expense is entitled to a partition suit to divide and sell the property in order to obtain compensation for the improvements.  However, if one places improvements without consent of the other cotenants, the amount of compensation is limited to the amount by which the value of the common property has been enhanced.

## Tenancy by the Entirety

In Virginia, tenancy by the entirety is similar to that described in the main text:  a special type of joint tenancy between husband and wife with no right to partition or to convey a half interest and indestructible except by divorce (which converts it to tenancy in common).

Property held by husband and wife as tenants by the entirety is legally an asset of both parties.  If one spouse *contracts* to convey property thus held, he or she cannot *convey* it and would be answerable to the would-be purchaser for subsequent inability to perform.  If a married woman has retained her maiden name, the deed should grant to "John Doe and Mary Jones, husband and wife, as tenants by the entirety," rather than "Mary Doe, a/k/a Mary Jones."

## Community Property

There are no "community property" laws in Virginia.

## LAND TRUST

In Virginia, a land trust is a trust in which the assets consist of real estate.  The deed to a trustee appears to confer full powers to deal with the real property and complete legal and equitable title to the trust property.  The trustee's powers, however, are restricted by a *trust agreement* mentioned in the deed in trust.  The agreement typically gives the beneficiary full powers of management and control; however, even the beneficiary cannot deal with the property as if no trust existed.  Such trusts generally continue for a definite term.

## TENANCY IN PARTNERSHIP

In Virginia, a partnership is able to own real property, but the individual partner's interest is considered personalty; no dower or curtesy rights arise.  A partner is co-owner with the other partners of real property as a tenant in partnership.  Tenancy in partnership has the following features:

1.   A partner (subject to the partnership agreement) has an equal right with the other partners to possess the property for partnership purposes but may not possess it for any other purpose without the other partners' consent.

2.   A partner's right in a property is not assignable unless all the partners assign their rights in the same property.

3.   A partner's right in the property is not subject to creditors, except for a claim against the partnership itself.  When partnership property is *attached* for a partnership debt, no rights can be claimed under homestead exemption laws by any partner (nor by the representative of a deceased partner).

4.   On the death of a partner, his interest in partnership property passes to the surviving partner(s) unless he was the last surviving partner, in which case his right in the property vests in his or her legal representative.  The surviving partner(s) or legal representative has no right to possess the property for other than a partnership purpose.

5.   The partner's right to partnership property is not subject to dower, curtesy or allowances to widows, heirs or next of kin.

A partner can transfer property on behalf of all the partners if acting within the scope of the firm's business and for firm purposes.  Partners may transfer partnership property among themselves, provided all partners consent.

Whenever a real estate licensee represents a buyer in purchasing property owned by a partnership, he should review a copy of the partnership agreement and make sure that a general partner with power to bind all other general partners executes the deed of conveyance.  Further, it is desirable to have a written resolution of the partnership authorizing the sale of the real property.

## CORPORATIONS

A corporation has the power to acquire and convey real property in its corporate name.  A contract entered into by a corporation under an assumed name may be enforced by either party.  If an instrument bears (1) a corporate seal and (2) proper signatures of corporate officers, it is presumed that it is a corporate instrument, even if the required *number* of signatures is lacking and it lacks the corporate name.  A purchaser of real estate from a corporation should always require a written corporate resolution duly authorizing the sale of property by the corporation.

## COOPERATIVE OWNERSHIP

Cooperative ownership is governed by the Virginia Real Estate Cooperative Act.  A cooperative is defined as "real estate owned by an association, each of the members of which is entitled, by virtue of his ownership interest in the association, to exclusive possession of a unit." Possession is by proprietary lease. A cooperative has common elements and limited common elements; it is created by a "declaration of cooperative" filed in the clerk's office of the circuit court where the real estate is located.

By Virginia statute, the cooperative association may adopt and amend bylaws, rules and regulations; adopt and amend budgets; hire and discharge management agents; regulate the use, maintenance and repair of common elements; impose charges; and exercise other powers conferred by the declaration and bylaws.

Before execution of a contract for sale of a cooperative interest, the purchaser must be given (among other things) a proprietary lease, a copy of the declaration and bylaws, the rules and regulations of the association and a certificate that shows the following:

1.   A statement disclosing the effect of any right of first refusal or other restraint on the transferability of the cooperative interest

2.   A statement of the amount of the monthly common expense assessment, as well as any unpaid expense currently due or payable from the sale and from the lessee

3.   A statement of any other fees payable by proprietary lessees

4.   A statement of any capital expenditures anticipated by the association for the current and next two succeeding fiscal years

5.   A statement of the amount of reserves for capital expenditures and any portions of them designated for specific projects

6.   The most recent regularly prepared balance sheet and income/expense statement, if any, of the association

7.   The current operating budget of the association and other pertinent information

It is typically the obligation of the real estate professional to obtain this information and furnish it to the purchaser.

Usually, a proposed purchaser of a cooperative unit must have the approval of the board of directors of the association. The real estate licensee should realize that because the cooperative owner owns stock in the cooperative and the cooperative actually owns the property, it is often difficult for the unit purchaser to obtain a mortgage or deed of trust to finance the purchase; most lenders require real estate for collateral for their loans.

## Condominium Ownership

"Condominium" means a system of separate ownership of individual units in multiunit projects. Virginia's Horizontal Property Act (1962) was one of the first state statutes allowing such ownership. The Condominium Act, which in 1974 superseded the 1962 Act, is designed to serve two purposes. It provides condominium developers the opportunity to take advantage of the flexibility in the concept of condominium, and it provides purchasers a greater measure of protection than the earlier law.

For a condominium to exist, the developer must record in the clerk's office of the circuit court where the property is located, various documents such as a declaration of condominium, bylaws, exhibits, schedules and/or certifications. In addition, a condominium "declarant" must register the project with the Real Estate Board. Prior to such registration, no interest in a condominium unit may be sold or offered for sale. The declaration of condominium must include the name of the project (including the word "condominium" or followed by the words "a condominium"), the name of the city where the project is located, a metes-and-bounds legal description and a description of common or limited common elements (and allocation of an undivided interest in these elements to each unit). Plats of survey of the property must be recorded along with the declaration, showing lot size as well as existing and/or planned improvements. The real estate professional should make sure a purchaser receives this information.

The unit owners' association, which manages the condominium, must hold meetings, elect officers and levy necessary charges and assessments; it can place a lien on any unit for unpaid assessments. The lien, once perfected, is prior to all other liens and encumbrances except real estate taxes, encumbrances recorded prior to the declaration and first deeds of trust recorded prior to the recording of the assessment lien. Since unpaid condominium assessments and dues (and association dues) constitute a lien against the unit in proportion to the liability of each owner, the real estate agent should verify that all dues are paid up and current to the date of closing. If a unit is sold by a person other than the developer, the unit owner must obtain certain information from the unit owners' association and furnish it to the purchaser before closing.

This must include a statement of capital expenditures anticipated by the unit owners' association, a statement of financial condition, insurance information, a copy of the current bylaws and other information.

The unit owners' association has limited authority; for example, it may not make repairs to an individual unit and assess the owner for the cost of the repairs without the owner's consent.

Virginia statute requires the person creating the condominium to warrant or guarantee each unit against structural defects for two years from the date it was conveyed, and all common elements for two years. Each unit must be warranted fit for habitation and constructed in a workmanlike manner.

If there is no unit owner other than the person creating the condominium, the declarant may unilaterally terminate the condominium or amend the condominium instruments. If there is any unit owner other than the declarant, then the condominium can be terminated only by agreement of four-fifths of the unit owners (or a larger majority if specified by the condominium instruments). If there is any unit owner other than the declarant, the condominium instruments can be amended only by agreement of two-thirds of the unit owners.

### Time-Shared Ownership

In Virginia, time-shared ownership is governed by the Virginia Real Estate Time-Share Act. Two types of time-shares are recognized. "Time-share estate" means a right to occupy a unit (or any of several units) during five or more separated time periods over a period of at least five years, including renewal options, coupled with *either* a freehold interest *or* an estate for years (lease) in a time-share project (or a specified portion of it).

"Time-share use" means a similar right, but *not* coupled with a freehold estate or an estate for years. Time-share use does not mean a right subject to a first-come, first-served, space-available basis such as exists in a country club, motel, health spa or similar facility.

In Virginia, a time-shared estate constitutes (for purposes of title) a separate estate or interest in a unit. The time-share instruments for each project must contain (1) the name of the project, which must include or be followed by the words "time-share"; (2) a legal descriptionsufficient to identify the project; (3) the form of time-share program (time-share *estate* or time-share *use*); and (4) the formula, fraction or percentage of any common expenses and voting rights assigned to each time-share.

By statute, there must be a time-share estate owners' association with authority to pass special assessments against unit owners. The association can place a lien on any time-share estate in the project for unpaid assessments. Time-shares may be terminated *only* by written agreement of time-share owners having at least 51 percent of the time-shares, or by a larger percentage if the time-share instrument so provides.

In Virginia, a developer must supply to any prospective purchaser a public offering statement, which fully discloses the characteristics of the time-share project and the time-shares offered, as well as all material circumstances affecting the time-share project. A purchaser of a time-share estate has the right to cancel the purchase contract until midnight of the seventh calendar day following the execution of the contract or receipt of the public offering statement, whichever is later. In the event of resale of a time-share by an owner other than the developer, the owner must obtain certain information from the developer, managing agent or time-share estate owners' association and furnish it to the purchaser prior to the execution of the time-share agreement and certificate of resale. This information must include (1) a statement disclosing the effect on the proposed purchaser of any right of first refusal or other restraint on transfer of the time-share or any portion of it; (2) a copy of the time-share instruments, bylaws, rules and regulations; and (3) a copy of the current budget or statement of capital expenditures. Like condominiums, time-shares are governed by authority of the Real Estate Board; thus, a developer may not offer or convey any interest in a time-share program unless it has been properly registered with the REB.

## QUESTIONS

1.    Bob, Jane and Ed are tenants in common of a parcel of real property; Ed sells the parcel to Darlene. What is true of this situation?

    a.    Darlene is now a tenant in common with Bob and Jane.
    b.    Darlene owns the parcel in severalty.
    c.    Bob or Jane can void the contract, but Ed is bound.
    d.    The contract is void: no one is bound, nothing conveys.

2.    In Virginia, how is a joint tenancy created?

    a.    By an act of the parties
    b.    By operation of law
    c.    By dissolution of a tenancy in common
    d.    By deed stating "as joint tenants and not tenants in common"

3.    Samuel Spade and Jacob Astor own property as joint tenants; Spade dies.  Does Mrs. Spade receive all or part of the property?

    a.    She receives a one-third fee simple interest (dower).
    b.    She receives Samuel's entire share.
    c.    Dower does not apply; she receives no share.
    d.    She can renounce Sam's will to receive the property.

4.    Grandy and Bagnall own real property as joint tenants; Grandy dies owing money to creditors.  What is the situation now?

    a.    Bagnall owns the property but is liable to the creditors.
    b.    Bagnall owns the property and is not liable to the creditors.
    c.    Bagnall owns the property except for a share owned by the creditors that represents the debts' percentage of the property value.
    d.    Mrs. Grandy owns the property interest formerly held by her husband and is liable for the debts.

5.    Which of the following is not true of partition in Virginia?

    a.    It may follow an accounting to verify whether one cotenant has received more than a fair share of profit.
    b.    It may apply if one cotenant has improved the property and wishes to be compensated for the improvements.
    c.    If a cotenant improves the property without the other cotenants' consent, the partition may not yield full value for the improvements.
    d.    If a joint tenant conveys his or her share to a third person and creates a tenancy in common, partition is no longer available to the remaining cotenants.

6.    Bill and Mary Smythe, husband and wife, own land as tenants by the entirety.  In a fit of pique, Bill signs a contract to sell his share of the property to James Twitt, his wife's worst enemy.  What is true concerning this transaction?

    a.    Bill cannot sell his half-interest.
    b.    While the contract appears valid, Bill cannot perform.
    c.    James Twitt could hold Bill answerable for his inability to perform under the contract.
    d.    All of the above

7.    Which of the following is not true of a tenancy in partnership?

    a.    No partner may use the property for a nonpartnership purpose without the other partners' consent.
    b.    Any partner's right in the property is assignable unless specifically forbidden in the deed.
    c.    A partner's right in the property is not subject to creditors (except for a claim against the partnership).
    d.    The partner's right to partnership property is not subject to dower, curtesy or allowances to surviving spouses or heirs.

8.   Which of the following is not necessary in order for a corporation to convey property by deed?

    a.   Corporate seal
    b.   Proper signatures of corporate officers
    c.   Corporate name and required number of signatures
    d.   None of the above

9.   When the real estate licensee is trying to sell a cooperative interest to a purchaser, which of the following might be considered misrepresentation?

    a.   "It won't be any trouble to get a mortgage on your unit."
    b.   "Even if you like this unit, you may not get it, because the Board of Directors still has to vote on your application."
    c.   "Before you sign anything, I have to get several documents for you to inspect."
    d.   "You realize that in purchasing this unit you're not actually buying real estate."

10.  If a condominium unit owner fails to pay the owners' association's assessment against his unit, what can the owner's association do?

    a.   Place a lien against the unit.
    b.   Garnish the owner's wages.
    c.   Nothing; as a stockholder, the unit owner has priority.
    d.   Revoke the unit owner's privileges and rights.

11.  Which of the following is *not* a recognized form of time-share in Virginia?

    a.   Time-share use
    b.   Time-share estate
    c.   Time-share fee
    d.   None of the above

12.  When the owner's interest in a time-share includes either a freehold interest or an estate for years, it is what type?

    a.   Time-share use
    b.   Time-share estate
    c.   Time-share fee
    d.   Time-share demise

13.  How long does the purchaser of a time-share have the right to cancel his purchase contract?

    a.   He cannot cancel it.
    b.   He has three business days.
    c.   He has seven calendar days.
    d.   He has two years.

14.    What is true of community property laws in Virginia?

    a.   The Virginia statute is patterned after California's.
    b.   Virginia recognizes only some community property provisions.
    c.   Dower and curtesy are community property provisions.
    d.   There are no community property laws in Virginia.

## ANSWERS

1. c. A contract by one tenant in common conveying the whole estate is voidable by the other cotenants, but the contracting cotenant may be bound to the contract.

2. a. Answer d is incorrect because Virginia does not recognize the right of survivorship unless it is explicitly stated in the instrument of conveyance.

3. c.

4. b. Deceased's creditors have no claim against survivors.

5. d.

6. d.

7. b.

8. c.

9. a.

10. a.

11. c.

12. b.

13. c.

14. d.

# 9

# Legal Descriptions

This chapter examines various methods by which boundaries of real property are described. Thorough and accurate descriptions of the property to be conveyed or subdivided are essential in the sales contract as well as in the documents transferring title. A survey is used to show the location and dimensions of the parcel as well as improvements.

## METHODS OF DESCRIBING REAL ESTATE

In Virginia, the most common method of describing real estate is a combination of the meets-and-bounds and lot-and-block methods.

The main text pointed out that the real estate licensee should use great care in describing property and should check both the real estate plat map and tax records as well as at least one deed by which the land was conveyed in the past to verify the proper legal description.

The description should enable the parties--or a court--to determine what land was intended to be conveyed. Evidence of surrounding facts and circumstances well known in that community at the time the deed was made is proper if it becomes necessary for a court to determine what property was meant to be conveyed. Disputed boundaries between two adjoining lands may be settled by express agreement. Virginia also provides for a court proceeding to establish a boundary line.

In Virginia, description of land by any of the following methods is legally sufficient if the county or city and state are given:

1. By courses and distances with an identifiable starting point

2. As bounded by natural or artificial objects or by the land of named persons

3. By reference to a recorded map, plat, survey, deed or other writing

4. By number or code on a recorded subdivision

5. By house number and named street where there is an established plan of numbering

6. By any name by which the land is generally known and by which it can be identified

7. As occupied or acquired by a named person at a definite time

8. As being all the land of the grantor in a designated way or acquired in a specific way

An example of a property description is set forth below:

> All those certain lots, pieces or parcels of land, situated in the city of Norfolk, Virginia, known numbered and designated on the Plat of Estabrook Corporation, made by S. W. Armistead, C.E., February 1920, and recorded in the clerk's office of the Circuit Court of the City of Chesapeake, Virginia, in Map Book 17, page 4, as Lots No. 35 and 36, located on the North side of Amherst Street in Block "E" in said Subdivision known as Estabrook, and appurtenances thereunto belonging, said lots being 25 x 100 feet each.

A shortened form of description is frequently used in listing agreements and sales contracts:

> Lots 35 and 36, Block E, Plat of Estabrook, Norfolk, Virginia 23513, also known and described as 3612 Amherst Street.

A false description does not invalidate the deed if after rejecting the false description enough remains to permit reliable identification of the land to be conveyed. A complete description such as the one above can be found in the deed conveying the property to the seller; the identical description should be used to convey the land to the buyer.

In conflicts concerning true boundaries, definite rules have been established giving preference to certain methods of description. Virginia observes the following order:

1. Natural monuments or landmarks
2. Artificial monuments and established lines, marked or surveyed
3. Adjacent boundaries or lines of adjoining tracts
4. Calls for courses and distances
5. Designation of quantity

This order is not inflexible and will not be applied where doing so would frustrate the intent of the parties to the conveyance.

Quantity is the least reliable method of describing land. Therefore, a description by acreage is inferior to all other deed descriptions.

In disputes among purchasers of lots shown on a plat, the metes and bounds established by accurate survey and corresponding calls of courses and distances noted on the plat will supersede pictorial errors in the plat and will control the dimensions and configuration of the lots.

## SURVEYING AND SURVEYS

The practice of land surveying includes surveying areas to determine their description, establishment (or reestablishment) of internal and external land boundaries and determination of topography, contours and location of physical improvements. Surveying also includes land planning and subdivisions, as well as preparation of plans and profiles for roads, streets and sidewalks.

In Virginia, a lender may not require a particular surveyor to perform the survey in connection with making a loan to purchase real property.  To engage in the practice of land surveying, a person must hold a valid surveyor's license unless exempted by the statute.  Therefore, a real estate licensee should never engage in the practice of surveying land.  Surveys are recorded in the clerk's office of the circuit court where the land is located.

The rectangular or government survey method is not frequently utilized in Virginia; however, the state has established the Virginia Coordinate System, which can use the system of coordinates established by the National Ocean Survey/National Geodetic Survey for defining the positions or locations of points within the Commonwealth.  Use of the systems is not compulsory in Virginia and is rarely utilized in real estate transactions.

## QUESTIONS

1.    Which of the following would be the least satisfactory legal description?

    a.    Lot 7, Block D, Plat of Colonial Valley
    b.    77.5 Acres, Seaside Neck
    c.    727 Oleander Drive, Fletcher's Falls, Virginia
    d.    Proceeding 120 feet due west of the intersection of the east line of Jackson Street and the north line of 11th street to a point; thence north 10 degrees 31 minutes west 100 feet

2.    A deed conveys property, naming it as "Lots 17 and 18, Block FF, Section 3, Plat of Greyflood Boundaries, otherwise known and described as 1416 Grey Havens Drive, Venusville, VA."  Research shows that Block FF has only 16 lots, and the street address given actually corresponds to Lot 16.  Does the deed still transfer property?

    a.    No; a false element in a description invalidates the deed.
    b.    No; since the lot description is faulty and a street address is insufficient, a new deed is needed.
    c.    Yes, as long as the buyer knows which property is meant.
    d.    Yes, since enough correct description remains to permit reliable identification of the property.

3.    John and Bill have bought neighboring lots in a new subdivision.  The pictorial representation of the lots shows that Bill's land reaches to a creek, while John's land falls just short of it.  At the closing, a survey of the lots shows a different angle from the street for the lots' boundary; the new line gives John creek access and denies it to Bill.  Who prevails here?

    a.    Bill does; the original pictorial representation governs.
    b.    Bill does, because otherwise the developer is guilty of misrepresentation.
    c.    John gets the creek access, because the survey supersedes pictorial errors in the plat.
    d.    A new survey must be drawn giving both buyers creek access.

4.    In Virginia, which of the following may *not* choose the individual surveyor to survey a parcel of land?

    a.    The broker, to help a seller sell a listing
    b.    The seller, to help the broker market the property
    c.    The buyer, to verify the location of land he or she will buy
    d.    The lender, in preparation for granting a deed of trust loan.

## ANSWERS

1.    b.    Descriptions by quantity have lowest priority with respect to reliability.

2.    d.    Normally a street address, though not the preferred description, is sufficient if the city has an established plan of numbering.

3.    c.

4.    d.

# 10

# Real Estate Taxes and Other Liens

This chapter will focus on liens that affect the ownership of real property. These liens may take the form of real property taxes, state taxes, liens created to protect a person who supplies labor or material in the construction of improvements on property, vendors' liens and others. In the event the lien is not satisfied, the owner's property may be sold in order to satisfy the lien.

## LIENS

A debt becomes a lien on the property of the debtor when it becomes a judgment or is secured by a deed of trust. A lien that the law would normally imply may be excluded if a contract expressly relinquishes the right to the lien.

An equitable lien may arise from a written contract, or it may be declared by a court of equity. The lien must rest upon a contract, express or implied; moral obligations alone will not sustain an equitable lien.

Various liens are created by statute in Virginia Code. Strict compliance with the statutes is necessary to create and enforce statutory liens. A suit to enforce a lien generally must be filed within a specific period of time or the lien will be waived. Before the court directs the sale of a debtor's lands to discharge liens, it should ascertain the name of each lienor, the amount (with interest) of each lien and its character and priority. In Virginia, liens attach to the property and "run with the land" rather than follow the individual owner of the property. Therefore, before conveying the property to a purchaser, it is critical to ascertain the liens against the property.

## TAX LIENS

Taxation is a statutory creation. A property tax is a charge on the owner of property by reason of his ownership alone, without regard to any use that may be made of it. The power of taxation is unlimited except as restricted by the state and federal constitutions.

The property to be taxed must be properly and accurately listed for taxation and books kept for that purpose that are open to the public to inform anyone interested in the property (including the owner) of the amount of tax. Note that the status of tax payments--i.e., whether or not they are current--may in some instances not be available to the public. The property must be valued or assessed. Upon evaluation, the tax is levied according to the proportion designated by tax laws. The constitutional requirement of uniformity of taxation means that all property of the same class must be taxed alike. However, this restriction does not prevent differences in taxation or the classification for taxation purposes of properties according to use in a business, trade or occupation. Uniform taxation requires uniformity both in the *rate* of taxation and in the *mode of assessment* on the taxable valuation and must be extended throughout the county, city, town or other district to which it applies.

## Exemptions From Real Estate Taxes

In Virginia, certain real estate is exempt from taxation. Burying grounds and lots used exclusively for burial purposes owned by a cemetery company or by lot owners are exempt from taxation. The Virginia Constitution exempts from state and local taxation "real estate and personal property owned and exclusively occupied or used by churches or religious bodies for religious worship or for the residences of their ministers." Also exempted is "property owned by public libraries or by institutions of learning not conducted for profit, so long as such property is primarily used for literary, scientific or educational purposes or purposes incidental thereto." The Virginia Constitution exempts "property used by its owner for religious, charitable, patriotic, historical, benevolent, cultural or public park and playground purposes." The controlling factor is the use of the private property in determining whether it is exempt from taxation. Public property may be exempted from taxation without regard to its use.

## Assessment

An *assessment* consists of listing property and placing a value on it to which the rate fixed by the levy is to be applied. In Virginia, all assessments of real estate must be at their fair market value. The common *legal* definition of fair market value as used by assessors is the price property will bring when offered for sale by a seller who desires but is not obligated to sell and bought by a buyer under no necessity of purchasing. While the Virginia Constitution requires that all assessments be made at fair market value, most local taxing authorities use a fixed multiple or percentage of the fair market value in order to arrive at the assessed value. The assessment should reflect its fair market value and be uniform within its class. There are many factors to be considered in arriving at the fair market value of property, including size, cost of the property, location, appearance, availability for use and the economic situation in the area, as well as other circumstances. Where there has been a recent sale of the property, of course, such sale should be considered.

The Virginia statute provides that a commissioner of revenue may make a supplemental assessment for the then current year. Therefore, when checking taxes it will be necessary to determine whether a supplemental assessment has been made on the property.

Under the Virginia statute, a circuit court may determine the correction of an erroneous assessment. There is a clear presumption that the assessment is valid, which can only be rebutted by showing manifest error or total disregard of controlling evidence.

As between a vendor (seller) and vendee (buyer) of property, the taxes run with the land, and the buyer is responsible for the payment of real estate taxes for the then current tax year from the *date of purchase* until the end of the year (i.e., the buyer is said to own the property on the date of settlement in Virginia). Taxes should be prorated between the vendee and vendor as of the date of the sale. Any delinquent taxes should be paid by the vendor at closing. Virginia statutes provide for the payment of penalties and interest on delinquent taxes.

Unpaid taxes on the property constitute a lien against it; therefore, the real estate licensee must verify with the seller that taxes for prior years have been paid and should ascertain the status of the current year's taxes. Any other pertinent tax information should be obtained from city or county tax offices.

The prior-year taxes must be paid by the seller at closing. The real estate professional may be faced with four phases of current taxes: (1) taxes not yet due and payable, (2) taxes currently due and payable, (3) taxes prepaid and (4) taxes past due. Taxes are not generally payable in advance of the due date. Each city and county has its own particular manner of assessing taxes and setting the due date. The taxes for the first phase, those not yet due and payable, are usually not paid at closing. The real estate professional's concern is the proration between seller and purchaser and the lender's instructions as to any escrow deposits.

As to taxes in the second and fourth phases, however, the closing attorney will normally collect these from the parties and pay them to the proper tax officials. If a sale is involved, the closing attorney will also normally prorate the current-year taxes between seller and purchaser. As to taxes in the third phase, those prepaid by the seller, the taxes are prorated, with the seller receiving a credit on the closing statement for the proration paid for the period of the purchaser's ownership. Proration (in the first and third phases) between purchaser and seller means essentially that each owns the property for a certain part of the year and each should pay the taxes for that period of ownership. Most contracts of purchase provide for proration.

Whenever past-year taxes cannot be used as an estimate for current taxes, the real estate professional must use whatever information is available to determine a reasonable estimate of the current accrued year's taxes. For example, when new construction has occurred the taxes on the land are prorated based on taxes for the past year. Taxes on the new improvements are estimated using the purchase price multiplied by the county or city assessment rate. Taxes are estimated from the date of the certificate of occupancy, or partial assessment may be levied against new construction not yet completed. If the closing is significantly later than the date of the certificate of occupancy or the closing date in the sales contract, the real estate professional should check to see if the property with the improvements has been reassessed.

As a general rule, the landlord under any ordinary lease is responsible for the taxes on the property, but this does not apply to a perpetual leaseholder who is in effect the rightful owner of the property and is entitled to its use forever. In such a case, the burden of taxation is placed on the lessee.

## Enforcement of Tax Liens

Under Virginia law, delinquent real property taxes are both a personal debt and a lien against the land. The tax lien on land has priority over all other liens except court costs. Thus, it overrides a vendor's lien even though the latter arose first. A tax lien is also prior to the landlord's lien for rent upon property on leased premises (see Landlord's Lien). The Virginia statutes give real estate taxes priority over a deed of trust in the distribution of proceeds under a foreclosure sale. The foreclosing trustee must satisfy all outstanding tax deficiencies before distributing the remaining proceeds and if the statute is not complied with, the delinquent taxes remain a debt against the purchaser at the sale.

A lien in favor of the United States for unpaid taxes, interest and penalties may arise against all real and personal property belonging to a taxpayer. The lien is perfected under Virginia law by filing notice of a tax lien in the circuit court for the jurisdiction in which the taxpayer resides; it remains in effect until the taxes are paid.

When taxes on real estate in a county, city or town are delinquent on December 31 following the third anniversary of the date on which the taxes became due, the real estate may be sold to collect the tax. At least 30 days before taking any action to sell the property, the tax collecting officer must send a notice to the last known address of the property owner. Notice of the sale must be published in a newspaper of general circulation in the locality, 30 to 60 days prior to the date on which the proceedings are to commence. The sale proceedings are initiated by filing a suit in the circuit court of the county or city where the real estate is located. The owner(s) of the real estate or any heirs, successors and assigns have the right to *redeem* the real estate *prior* to the sale date by paying the court all taxes, penalties and interest due, plus costs (including cost of publication and a reasonable attorney's fee set by the court).

The former owner (including heirs or assigns) of any real estate sold for delinquent real estate taxes is entitled to any receipts from the sale in excess of the taxes, penalties, interest and costs.

## Special Assessments

Virginia law makes a distinction between special assessments (special taxes to pay for local improvements) and general tax levies for purposes of carrying on the government. Special assessments are founded upon the theory of benefits brought about by improvements to the adjacent property. This benefit enhances the value of the specific property because of a public improvement and is distinguished from general benefits to the entire community. In Virginia, a statute specifically provides that notice must be given to abutting landowners of the contemplated improvements before the ordinance authorizing the improvements is put into effect. This gives the landowner an opportunity to be heard concerning the adoption or rejection of such an ordinance.

The statute provides for special assessments relating to sewers, street paving and other local public improvements. The only property subject to a special assessment is that of abutting landowners. Local improvements may be ordered by a town or city council (with costs to be defrayed by special assessment) on a petition from not less than three-fourths of the landowners to be affected by the assessment. However, the council may issue such an order without a petition. The Virginia statute provides simply that the amount of special assessment for a local improvement constitutes a lien on the property benefited by the improvement, and the lien is enforceable by a suit in court. Property owners have the right to appear before the municipal authorities and protest both the authorization of the improvements and the assessments.

## LIENS OTHER THAN TAXES

## Mechanics' Liens

Anyone in Virginia who performs labor or furnishes material of the value of $50.00 or more for the construction, removal, repair or improvement of any building or structure has a right of lien upon the land and building or structure. The object of the law is to give laborers and materialmen the security of a lien on the property to the extent that they have added to its value. A general contractor or a subcontractor may perfect a mechanic's lien by filing a *memorandum of mechanic's lien* and an affidavit with the clerk of court where the building or structure is located within 90 days of the last day of the month in which the contractor last performed labor or furnished materials. However, in no event can filing occur later than 90 days from the time the building is completed or the work otherwise terminated. A subcontractor must also give written notice to the owner of the property. A memorandum of mechanic's lien is recorded in the deed books in the clerk's office where the property is located. The memorandum generally contains the name of the owner of the property sought to be charged, the name of the claimant of the lien, the amount of the claim, the time when the amount is or will be due and payable and a brief description of the property on which the lienor claims a lien.

A mechanic's lien is enforced by a suit filed within six months of recording the memorandum of lien or 60 days from the completion or termination of work on the structure, whichever is later. If the person who ordered the work owns less than the fee simple estate in the land, only the interest he has is subject to the lien.

When the vendee (buyer) under a contract of sale of real estate causes a building or structure to be erected or repaired before closing on the land to be conveyed and the owner has actual knowledge of the erection or repairs, the interests of the owner are subject to the lien. By Virginia statue, when a lien (e.g., a deed of trust) is created on land *before* work for which the mechanic's lien is claimed began or materials furnished, the deed of trust is the first lien on the land and a second lien on the building or structure. A deed of trust recorded before the work began is entitled to priority to the extent of the estimated value of the property without the improvements for which the lien is claimed.

Typically, at closing a seller must execute an affidavit stating that no work has been performed or any materials furnished within 120 days before the date of closing in order to ensure that no mechanic could file a lien against the property *after* closing for labor performed or materials furnished *before* closing.

In addition, with regard to new construction, the real estate professional should demand a *lien waiver* executed by the general contractor and all subcontractors that states all amounts have been paid for labor performed and materials furnished in connection with the construction of the building or structure.

## Judgments

Every money judgment rendered in Virginia by any state or federal court or by confession of judgment constitutes a lien on real estate owned now or in the future by the judgment debtor. The lien is effective from the date the judgment is *docketed* (i.e., indexed by the clerk of court of the city or county where the real estate is situated). If the judgment debtor does not currently own real estate but his parents or siblings do, and the location of the real estate is known, it is wise to docket the judgment in that locality in case the real estate passes to the debtor upon the death of the owner. If the judgment is obtained in a circuit court, the clerk of that court will automatically docket the judgment in that court.

An execution may be issued and the judgment enforced within 20 years from the date the judgment was rendered. A judgment may be extended beyond its 20-year life by a motion made in the circuit court, following notice to the judgment debtor. It is necessary to redocket the judgment.

If the real estate is conveyed to a grantee for value subject to a judgment lien, the judgment creditor must bring the suit to enforce the judgment lien within ten years from the date of recordation of the deed to the grantee.

If the judgment is for recovery of specific real property, a writ of possession is needed in Virginia. If it is discovered that the judgment debtor owns real estate outside Virginia, it is possible to require the debtor to convey it to a sheriff.

Within 30 days of the satisfaction of a judgment, a judgment creditor is required to release the judgment wherever docketed. Failure to do so within ten days of demand by the judgment debtor makes the creditor liable for a fine up to $50.

## Estate and Inheritance Tax Liens

A lien arises upon all property, real and personal, located in the Commonwealth of Virginia of every decedent having a taxable estate who fails to pay the tax imposed by the Virginia Estate Tax Act. In the case of a nonresident decedent having a taxable estate, the lien arises automatically at death. In the case of a resident decedent, the liens attach to the real estate only when a memorandum is filed by the Department of Taxation in the clerk's office of the county or city where such real estate is located. The lien, once it attaches, is enforceable for ten years from the date of death of the decedent. The tax imposed is a *succession tax* rather than an estate tax; the tax is upon the right to *succeed* to the property or an interest in it, not to *transmit* it. The tax is not levied on the *property* of which an estate is composed, but upon the shifting of economic benefits and the privilege of transmitting or receiving such benefits.

## Attachments

The mere issuance of an attachment creates no lien on the real estate, since in order to create a lien it is necessary for the officer to show that levy (actual attachment or seizure) was made.

## Lis Pendens

A *lis pendens*, or pending suit, does not bind or affect a subsequent purchaser of real estate unless a memorandum is properly recorded, setting forth the title of the suit, the general object of the suit, the court where it is pending, the amount of the claim, a description of the property and the name of the person whose estate is intended to be affected. If the lis pendens is not docketed as provided by the statutes, a purchaser without notice of the pending suit takes good title, with no lien on the land by virtue of the pending suit.

## Vendor's Lien

Virginia statute provides that if any person conveys any real estate and the purchase money remains unpaid at the time of the conveyance, the vendor will *not* have a lien for the unpaid purchase money, *unless* the lien is expressly reserved on the face of the deed. The object of this statute is to make the lien a matter of record and thus furnish to all persons dealing with the property the necessary information of all liens and encumbrances on the property. The extent of the vendor's lien does not depend upon the extent of the vendor's interest in the land conveyed, but upon the contract of the parties as gathered from the deed itself in reserving the lien.

## Landlord's Lien

The Virginia statutes give a landlord a right of lien that is fixed and specific.  It exists independently of the right of holding property for payment of recent (attachment), which is merely a remedy for enforcement.  When the landlord's lien for rent is obtained, it relates back to the beginning of the tenancy and takes precedence over any lien that any other person has obtained or created against goods (personal property) on the leased premises after the beginning of the tenancy.  A lien legally attaches to all property on the preemies when the lien is asserted or on the premises within 30 days prior to attachment of lien.  The landlord can seize the tenant's goods only to the extent necessary to satisfy the rent justly believed to be due.

## QUESTIONS

1.  At which point does a debt become a lien against real property?

    a.  When the debt becomes owed
    b.  When a contract involving payment is signed
    c.  When it becomes a judgment or a deed of trust
    d.  When it is enforced

2.  Which of the following is required for an equitable lien?

    a.  A contract between the parties
    b.  A moral obligation to the injured party
    c.  Specific statutory authorization to impose the lien
    d.  Written commitment to pay lienor a sum of money

3.  Barbara's house is near the end of a block; right beside her house is Henry's Bakery on the corner lot.  How must these properties be treated for real estate tax purposes?

    a.  There can be no difference between them.
    b.  They may be differently classified according to use.
    c.  A sliding value scale may be applied to businesses, but not to residences, which are strictly *ad valorem*.
    d.  Since the bakery abuts a residential zone, it must be treated as a residence.

4.  Which of the following types of real property is exempt from real property taxation?

    a.  Burying grounds
    b.  Municipal or government-owned land
    c.  Land owned by nonprofit educational institutions
    d.  All of the above

5.   In Virginia, how do assessments for tax purposes compare to the property's market value?

   a.   Valuation is at local option, so there is no uniform statewide ratio.
   b.   The state constitution requires that all assessments be at fair market value.
   c.   The state constitution requires that all assessments be at the same percentage of fair market value (now 85 percent).
   d.   None of the above

6.   Once the annual tax assessment has been made, does it remain in force all year?

   a.   Yes.
   b.   Yes, except when a supplemental assessment is made.
   c.   No, unless a recertification has been done.
   d.   No; there is a statutory appreciation rate that must be applied after six months.

7.   In Virginia, who owns the property (for real estate tax purposes) on the date of sale?

   a.   The buyer owns it.
   b.   The seller owns it.
   c.   It is divided evenly, with each party paying half of the tax for that day.
   d.   This item must be negotiated on the sales contract.

8.   In Virginia, when real property is sold to satisfy a real estate tax lien, the buyer at the tax sale receives:

   a.   a certificate of sale.
   b.   a deed.
   c.   a cloud on title.
   d.   a certificate of equitable title.

9.   Janet is relieved to learn that her home, which up to now has had to rely on a septic tank for sewage disposal, will soon be served by a city sewer line.  How will this improvement most likely be paid for?

   a.   General real estate tax
   b.   Municipal bonds
   c.   Special assessment
   d.   State road-use tax

10.  How long after the work was done may the mechanic wait before filing a mechanic's lien?

   a.   No more than 30 days
   b.   No more than 60 days
   c.   No more than 90 days
   d.   No more than six months

11.   How soon after filing the lien must the mechanic enforce it by filing suit?

    a.   Within three months
    b.   Within six months
    c.   Within nine months
    d.   Within one year

12.   A deed of trust was recorded against a property in March of 1985, and a mechanic's lien was recorded for work on the house in March of 1988.  In this case, the priority of the deed of trust is:

    a.   first on building and land.
    b.   second on building and land.
    c.   first on the building, second on the land.
    d.   second on the building, first on the land.

13.   Within what period of time does a creditor on a judgment have to enforce the judgment once it is rendered?

    a.   Within six months
    b.   Within one year
    c.   Within five years
    d.   Within 20 years

## ANSWERS

1.   c.

2.   a.

3.   b.

4.   d.

5.   b.

6.   b.

7.   a.

8.   b.

9.   c.

10.   c.

11.   b.

12.   d.

13.   d.

# Real Estate Contracts

The Real Estate Board regulations touch on real estate contracts in two primary areas: records and deposits of funds, and grounds for disciplinary action.

## RECORDS AND DEPOSITS OF FUNDS

The real estate broker or rental location agent is required to keep accurate, detailed and complete records of all transactions conducted by the brokerage or agency. The real estate broker may maintain the records either at the firm's main place of business or at a designated branch office. Out-of-state firms doing business in real estate brokerage in Virginia must maintain records at the Virginia office of the firm.

The REB requires that the following information be shown in the records kept by the broker or rental location agent: when and from who money was received, date and place of deposit, and the final disposition of funds upon completion of the transaction.

Each firm must maintain in the firm's name at least one escrow or trust account (it may have more than one) into which all monies to be kept for others must be deposited. This account must be maintained in a federally insured depository in Virginia. Into this account should be placed the following categories of funds:

- Down payments

- Ernest money deposits

- Monies received at settlement of a transaction

- Rental payments

- Rental security deposits

- Money advanced by a buyer or seller to pay expenses connected with the closing of a transaction

- Money advanced by the broker's principal or expended upon the principal's behalf

- Any other escrow funds

Funds belonging to any of these categories *must* be deposited in the escrow account unless all parties to the transaction have agreed otherwise in writing ("all parties" includes buyer, seller and any real estate brokerage firms involved). The principal broker (or supervising broker of a branch office who has such an account) may be held responsible for the escrow account, both with respect to maintaining accurate records and to the actual funds entrusted to the broker to be kept in the account.

Although an earnest money deposit is not required by law, it is a normal and expected part of any offer on real property; as such it must be protected by placement in an account as described above.  Further, unless otherwise agreed by all parties to a transaction, the earnest money cannot be used for any other purpose.  The REB regulations single out as inappropriate such other uses as "expenses incidental to closing a transaction, e.g., fees for appraisal, insurance, credit report, etc."  The broker's bookkeeping system must be accurate and complete, so that the REB or its agents can verify full compliance with the regulations.

Funds may be withdrawn from the escrow account only under strictly defined circumstances.  Once a contract for the sale of real property has been accepted, the earnest money or down payment received by the brokerage firm must be placed in the escrow account and remain there until the transaction is consummated or terminated; if the transaction is not consummated, the funds must remain in escrow until one of three provisions is met:

1.    All parties to the transaction (buyer, seller, both brokers) have agreed to the disposition of the funds.  This is ordinarily accomplished through signing a buyer-seller release agreement or the equivalent.  In this agreement, the buyer's equitable title is specifically released, and the original sales contract is rescinded (in which case the buyer receives the earnest money) or forfeited (in which case the seller receives the earnest money, less-agreed on sum, which goes to the broker).  Even if the buyer receives his money back, the broker or seller may be entitled to reimbursement of certain expenses; these will be itemized on the release agreement.

2.    A court of competent jurisdiction orders disbursement of the funds.

3.    The broker can pay the funds to the party entitled to receive them, according to the clear and explicit terms of the contract that established the deposit.  This provision, which appeared for the first time in 1987 REB regulations, now permits and encourages the broker to include language in sales contracts for the specific purpose of addressing unconsummated transactions and the disbursement of earnest money deposits.  In complying with this regulation, the broker must notify each party who will not receive payment under these terms that the payment will be made.  The notification must be by hand delivery or regular or certified mail, and the recipient has 30 days to make a written protest to the broker.

Unless otherwise agreed by all parties to a transaction, no money may be taken from the earnest money deposit as commission until the transaction is consummated.  While the escrow account contains funds that may ultimately belong to the broker and his associates and salespeople, all such funds must be properly identified in the account records.  When the funds become due to the licensee, they must be paid to the firm by a check drawn on the escrow account.  Commingling of funds (broker having escrow and business funds in the same account) is not involved here so long as the account is an active one and not merely an interest-gathering savings account; the REB regulations specify that there must be "periodic withdrawals of said funds at intervals of not more than six months."  The broker must be able at any time to give an accurate account of the monies in the escrow that belong to the firm.

In Virginia, it is legal to keep escrow funds in an interest-bearing account, so long as written disclosure regarding disbursement of the interest is made to the principals in the transaction.

Ordinarily the interest belongs to the broker; however, many brokers choose to keep the funds in a noninterest-bearing account to save on bookkeeping costs.

Escrow funds may be used to purchase certificates of deposit. However, the certificate must remain within the direct control of the principal or supervising broker, so that the funds may be immediately disbursed to the party entitled to them in the event that the transaction isterminated prior to the expected closing date. The regulations specifically prohibit the broker from pledging, hypothecating or in any way relinquishing control of the certificate; these actions constitute commingling of funds and may result in the funds becoming unavailable to be disbursed to the party entitled to them if the transaction terminates at an unexpected time.

## GROUNDS FOR DISCIPLINARY ACTION

The regulations address three primary areas regarding written contracts: paragraph 3.5, section 10 addresses distribution of contract copies; sections 16-19 deal with written offers and sales contracts; and sections 24-27 deal with record-keeping and handling of funds.

The broker is subject to discipline for failing to make prompt delivery of complete and legible copies of each relevant document to each party concerned. Documents covered by this regulation include listings, sales contracts, residential leases and other agreements negotiated by the broker or his salespeople. "Prompt" means at the time of signature or as soon thereafter as practical.

The licensee must present to the seller, in a prompt and timely manner, every written offer to purchase obtained on the property the firm has listed. This includes offers that are received after the property is "under contract." It also includes offers written on forms other than those printed by the local multiple listing service or other local organization, as well as handwritten offers not presented on any form; of course, such offers must be handled with the extra degree of care accorded any unfamiliar circumstance. If an offer is received when the property is already under contract, the new offer must be dealt with as a "backup" offer. If accepted, it must be subject to removal of the prior contract and neither seller nor broker can do anything prejudicial to the consummation of the transaction outlined in the prior contract.

Once a contract has been fully executed (signed) by all parties to it, the broker must deliver signed copies to all the parties, so that everyone has in his possession a signed copy of the final version of the contract.

If any material change occurs in the circumstances relevant to a transaction, the broker must provide prompt written notice of the change to all parties. Such changes might include shifts in interest rate or points, buyer's decision to switch loan types or lenders, discovery of termite or other damage in the seller's property, or any circumstances of similar significance.

The broker is liable for disciplinary action if he fails to include the complete terms of the transaction in the offer, including identification of parties holding deposits. This regulation holds for both sale and rental transactions. Together with Regulation 31 under Grounds for Disciplinary Action, this regulation addresses the issue of "side agreements": items agreed to between any or all of the parties but not included in the sales contract. Commonly referred to as "gentlemen's agreements," "understandings," "handshakes," "side notes" and the like, these are agreements ordinarily designed to conceal a part of the purchase price from the lender.

Frequently they are not written down; as such, they are unenforceable under the statute of frauds. Often these agreements are contrary to provisions in the sales contract; as such, they are unenforceable under the parol evidence rule. When these items become known to the lender, they are ordinarily viewed as default in the deed of trust or mortgage and frequentlylead to foreclosure. The only safe and legal procedure is to reveal all terms and conditions of the contract in writing and to resist the temptation to "shade" a customer's qualifications or the property's purchase price to facilitate a transaction.

The broker must maintain complete and accurate records of receipts and disbursement of funds for three years after a transaction has closed. He can be disciplined for failing to account for or remit funds coming into his possession from others within a reasonable time.

When a written offer on a property is received by a licensee, it will ordinarily be accompanied by a check for the earnest money; less frequently, cash is included instead. These items may be routinely accepted by the licensee, and the offer may be presented to the seller without noting anything other than the amount in conversation with the seller (unless an unusual circumstance is present, such as a postdated check). However, if the offer is accompanied by a note, a non-negotiable instrument or anything of value not readily negotiable, the licensee may not accept it unless he acknowledges its acceptance in writing on the face of the contract. The licensee's acceptance of the unusual deposit is only for the purpose of presenting the offer to the seller; of course, the seller is under no obligation to accept the deposit (indeed, any deposit is a negotiable item). In the case of an "in-kind" deposit--a car, a yacht, a thoroughbred horse, for example--the item itself cannot be deposited in the broker's account. A note in the amount of the appraised value of the item should be deposited instead, with the item itself being kept safe in circumstances arrived at by mutual agreement.


## STATUTE OF FRAUDS


The only function of Virginia's Statute of Frauds is to prevent enforcement of an oral contract or promise. The statute is concerned with enforceability, not validity. It forbids bringing my action concerning a contract for sale of real estate or for a lease on real property for more than one year unless the contract or lease is in writing.

While an oral lease for a term of more than one year is unenforceable and the parties cannot be compelled to do so, they may still perform the agreement. In such a lease, the contract is void because neither party can compel the other to perform. Courts have held that the terms of the invalid lease will be considered as controlling in all respects except for the duration of the lease.


## SAMPLE RESIDENTIAL CONTRACT


A residential contract of purchase prepared by the Real Estate Committee of the Virginia Bar Association appears on pages 57-58. The licensee should be aware of the variety of local forms available for purchase contracts, listing agreements, leases and addendums for any or all of these. While any licensee in Virginia is legally permitted to practice real estate anywhere in the state, it is advisable to be familiar with local forms, procedures and customs before practicing in another area.

**Figure 11.1:** Sample Residential Purchase Contract

## RESIDENTIAL CONTRACT OF PURCHASE

*This is a suggested form of contract recommended by the Real Estate Committee of The Virginia Bar Association for use in the sale and purchase of existing residential property only. This form is not mandatory; other forms are available. You should determine if this form is appropriate for your transaction. It is a legally binding contract. If not understood, legal advice should be obtained before it is signed.*

THIS CONTRACT OF PURCHASE is made as of _____ , 19 ____ between _____ _____ , whose address is _____ , owner of record of the Property sold herein (the "Seller", whether one or more), and _____ whose address is _____ (the "Purchaser", whether one or more), and _____ ("Listing Broker"), and _____ ("Selling Broker").

1. **REAL PROPERTY.** Purchaser agrees to buy and Seller agrees to sell the land and all improvements thereon and appurtenances thereto and, if not fronting on a public road, a recorded and mortgageable right of way providing adequate access thereto (the "Property"), located in the County or City of _____ , Virginia, and described as:
Street Address _____
Legal Description _____
_____
_____
_____

2. **PERSONAL PROPERTY:** The following personal property is included in this sale: _____
_____
_____

3. **PURCHASE PRICE:** The purchase price is _____ Dollars ($ ____ ), payable as follows:
(a) $ _____ earnest money by (i) check to be held in escrow by Listing Broker until Settlement and then credited to Purchaser, or until this Contract is terminated and it is disbursed in accordance with Paragraph A of the Standard Provisions OR (ii) promissory note of Purchaser payable on _____ , 19 ____ , and held by Listing Broker in accordance with (i) above.

(b) $ _____ (approximately) by assumption of the unpaid principal balance and all obligations of Seller on the existing loan secured by a deed of trust on the Property, at an interest rate not exceeding _____ and an assumption fee not exceeding $ ____ .

(c) $ _____ [approximately if loan being assumed in (b)] by deferred purchase money financing of Seller secured by a ( _____ first) ( _____ second) deed of trust on the Property, bearing interest at the rate of _____ % per year, amortized over _____ years, payable in monthly installments of $ ____ , with a final payment _____ years after Settlement. A late payment fee of 5% will be charged on any payment not received within 15 calendar days after maturity. The debt may be prepaid in whole or in part without penalty at any time, and shall be subject to call in event of sale or transfer of the Property. The note shall be a negotiable instrument and the deed of trust shall be in statutory form, except to the extent otherwise agreed by Seller and Purchaser.

(d) $ _____ the balance of the purchase price in cash or by cashier's or certified check at Settlement.
$ _____ TOTAL PURCHASE PRICE (The total of a, b, c, and d above, as applicable).

4. **SETTLEMENT AND POSSESSION:** Settlement shall be made at _____ on _____ . 19 ____ ("Settlement"). Possession shall be given at Settlement, unless otherwise agreed in writing by the parties.

5. **REAL ESTATE COMMISSION:** Seller represents that he is party to a listing agreement with the Listing Broker pursuant to which the Listing Broker will be paid a fee of _____ % of the purchase price for services. From that fee, the Selling Broker shall receive a fee of $ ____ . Seller hereby authorizes and directs the settlement agent to disburse from the Seller's proceeds at Settlement the Selling Broker's fee and the Listing Broker's fee.

6. **CONDITIONS:** This Contract is contingent upon the following (check those applicable):
(a) Purchaser shall have obtained a written commitment for a ( ) conventional, ( ) V.A. ( ) FHA [select one] first deed of trust loan on the Property with a term of _____ years, bearing interest ( ) at a fixed rate not exceeding _____ % per year or ( ) at an adjustable rate with an initial rate not exceeding _____ % per year, and requiring not more than _____ discount points (excluding a loan origination fee of not more than _____ %), of which Seller agrees to pay _____ discount points.

(b) Other Conditions: _____
_____
_____
_____
_____

7. **OTHER TERMS:** _____
_____
_____
_____
_____

8. **STANDARD PROVISIONS ON REVERSE SIDE HEREOF:** All of the Standard Provisions on the REVERSE SIDE HEREOF are incorporated by reference and shall apply to this Contract except the following lettered Standard Provisions are hereby deleted: _____ . (If none are deleted, state "None" in this blank.)

9. **ACCEPTANCE:** This Contract when signed by Purchaser shall be deemed an offer and shall remain in effect, unless withdrawn, until _____ (time), _____ , 19 ____ . If not accepted within that time by Seller by delivery of a signed copy of this Contract to Purchaser or Purchaser's designated representative, it shall become null and void.

Seller accepts this Contract at _____ (time), _____ , 19 ____ .

_____
Seller

_____
Seller

_____
Purchaser

_____
Purchaser

I hereby acknowledge receipt
of the earnest money deposit
herein. ( ) check ( ) cash
( ) note
Date: _____

_____
Listing Broker

By: _____

_____
Selling Broker

By: _____

Figure 11.1:  Sample Residential Purchase Contract  (Continued)

---

### STANDARD PROVISIONS

A.  *EARNEST MONEY:* In the event this Contract is terminated as provided herein, or in the event of a breach of this Contract by Seller, the earnest money shall be returned to Purchaser, but such return shall not affect any other remedies available to Purchaser for Seller's breach. In the event Purchaser breaches this Contract, the earnest money shall be paid to Seller, but such payment shall not preclude any other remedies available to Seller for such breach.

The deposit shall be held in conformity with the regulations of the Virginia Real Estate Commission and other applicable law. If this Contract is not consummated and a dispute exists between Seller and Purchaser, the deposit will be held in escrow by the Listing Broker until the Seller and Purchaser have agreed to the disposition thereof, or a court of competent jurisdiction orders disbursement.

B.  *EXPENSES AND PRORATIONS:* Seller agrees to pay the expense of preparing the deed, certificates for non-foreign status and Form 1099-B and the recordation tax applicable to grantors. Except as otherwise agreed herein, all other expenses incurred by Purchaser in connection with this purchase, including, without limitation, title examination, insurance premiums, survey costs, recording costs, loan document preparation costs and fees of Purchaser's attorney, shall be borne by Purchaser. All taxes, assessments, interest, rent and mortgage insurance, if any, shall be prorated as of Settlement. In addition to the Purchase Price, Purchaser shall pay Seller (i) for all fuel oil remaining on the Property (if any) at the prevailing market price as of Settlement and (ii) any escrow deposits made by Seller which are credited to Purchaser by the holders thereof.

C.  *TITLE:* At Settlement, Seller shall convey to Purchaser good and marketable fee simple title to the Property by deed of general warranty containing English Covenants of title, free of all liens, defects and encumbrances, except as otherwise indicated herein, and subject only to such restrictions and easements as shall then be of record which do not affect the use of the Property for residential purposes or render the title unmarketable. If a defect is found which can be remedied by legal action within a reasonable time, Seller shall, at Seller's expense, promptly take such action as is necessary to cure the defect. If Seller, acting in good faith, is unable to have such defect corrected within 60 days after notice of such defect is given to Seller, then this Contract may be terminated by either Seller or Purchaser. Purchaser may extend the date for Settlement to the extent necessary for Seller to comply with this Paragraph.

In the event the Property is taxed under land use assessment and this sale results in disqualification from land use eligibility, Seller shall pay any rollback taxes assessed. If the Property continues to be eligible for land use assessment, Purchaser agrees to make application, at Purchaser's expense, for continuation under land use, and to pay any rollback taxes resulting from failure to file or to qualify.

D.  *RISK OF LOSS:* All risk of loss or damage to the Property by fire, windstorm, casualty or other cause, or taking by eminent domain, is assumed by Seller until Settlement. In the event of substantial loss or damage to the Property before Settlement, Purchaser shall have the option of either (i) terminating this Contract, or (ii) affirming this Contract, in which event Seller shall assign to Purchaser all of Seller's rights under any applicable policy or policies of insurance and any condemnation awards and pay over to Purchaser any sums received as a result of such loss or damage.

E.  *EQUIPMENT CONDITION AND INSPECTION:* Purchaser agrees to accept the Property at Settlement in its present physical condition, except as otherwise provided herein. Seller warrants that any appliances listed in Paragraph 2, the heating and cooling equipment, plumbing systems (including well and septic systems), electric systems and roof will be in working order at Settlement or at Purchaser's occupancy, whichever occurs first. Purchaser may have these elements inspected, at Purchaser's expense, provided such inspections are completed within 30 days after Seller signs this Contract. If defects are found by such inspections, Seller shall, at Seller's expense, promptly repair the defects. Seller agrees to deliver the Property in broom-clean condition and to exercise reasonable and ordinary care in the maintenance and upkeep of the Property between the date this Contract is executed by Seller and Settlement or at Purchaser's occupancy, whichever occurs first. Purchaser and his representatives shall have the right to make a further inspection immediately before Settlement or occupancy. Purchaser shall also have the right within such 30 days to inspect, at Purchaser's expense, for radon, asbestos and urea-formaldehyde and, if discovered, Seller shall timely cure such defect.

F.  *WELL AND SEPTIC:* If the Property is on well and/or septic systems, Seller agrees to furnish Purchaser with a certificate from the appropriate governmental authority, or mutually acceptable private company, indicating that the well water is potable and that there is no evidence of malfunction of the septic system. If either system is found defective, Seller shall take immediate steps to repair all defects at Seller's expense.

G.  *WOOD INFESTATION INSPECTION AND REPORT:* Seller shall deliver to Purchaser a report from a qualified licensed exterminator, dated not earlier than 30 days before Settlement, that the principal dwelling on the Property is free of infestation and structural damage from termites and other wood-destroying insects. If such insects are found, Seller shall, at Seller's expense, have the dwelling treated and damage repaired and shall furnish a one-year bond on such treatment work.

H.  *SELLER'S AND PURCHASER'S OPTION:* In the event that the total cost of fulfilling Seller's obligations in Paragraphs C, E, F and G above exceeds $750.00, Seller shall have the option to (a) pay the total costs or (b) pay $750.00 to Purchaser and refuse to pay any excess over that amount. If Seller elects (b), Purchaser shall have the option to (x) accept the Property in its present condition in which case Seller shall pay $750.00 to Purchaser at Settlement, or (y) terminate the Contract.

I.  *AFFIDAVITS AND CERTIFICATES:* Seller shall deliver to Purchaser an affidavit to the effect that no labor or materials have been furnished to the Property within the statutory period for the filing of mechanics' or materialmen's liens against the Property or, if labor or materials have been furnished, that the costs thereof have been paid. Seller shall also deliver to Purchaser the certificates required by Sections 1445 (FIRPTA) and 6045 (Form 1099-B) of the Internal Revenue Code.

K.  *VA/FHA LOAN:* If VA or FHA financing is selected in Paragraph 6(a), notwithstanding any other provisions of this Contract, Purchaser shall not incur any penalty by forfeiture of deposit or any other penalty, or be further obligated under this Contract unless there has been delivered to Purchaser a certificate issued by VA or FHA (whichever is applicable), setting forth the appraised value of the Property (exclusive of closing costs if FHA) of not less than the Purchase Price. Purchaser may proceed with this Contract without regard to the appraised value, and Seller may alter this Contract to reduce the Purchase Price to the appraised value, providing one or the other option is exercised in writing within 72 hours of receipt of the certificate of value. No appeal of the appraised value may be made without written mutual consent of Purchaser and Seller. Seller shall not be required to make any repairs required by VA or FHA unless provided for in Paragraph 7. Seller, in addition to paying the loan discount points provided for in Paragraph 3(c), agrees to pay all other fees required by VA or FHA to be paid by the Seller provided the total amount of such fees does not exceed $100.00. If HUD/FHA FINANCING APPLIES, THE APPRAISED VALUATION IS ARRIVED AT TO DETERMINE THE MAXIMUM MORTGAGE WHICH HUD/FHA WILL INSURE. HUD/FHA DOES NOT WARRANT THE VALUE OR THE CONDITION OF THE PROPERTY. THE PURCHASER SHOULD SATISFY HIMSELF/HERSELF THAT THE PRICE AND CONDITION OF THE PROPERTY ARE ACCEPTABLE.

L.  *CONDOMINIUM RESALE:* If this is a condominium resale, this Contract is subject to the Virginia Condominium Act (Section 55-79.39, et seq., Code of Virginia) which requires Seller to furnish certain financial and other disclosures to Purchaser before entering into a binding contract of sale. If the required disclosures are not yet available, Seller agrees to request same promptly from all unit owners associations and deliver them to Purchaser who agrees to acknowledge receipt upon delivery. If Seller fails to furnish Purchaser such disclosures within fifteen (15) days after the date of execution of this Contract by Seller or the disclosures are found to be unacceptable by the Purchaser upon receipt, Purchaser may terminate this Contract by notice thereof to Seller at the address set forth herein provided Purchaser does so within 72 hours after receipt or such 15-day period if not received.

M.  *ASSIGNABILITY:* This Contract may not be assigned by either Seller or Purchaser without the written consent of the other.

N.  *MISCELLANEOUS:* The parties to this Contract agree that it shall be binding upon them, and their respective personal representatives, successors and assigns; that its provisions shall be merged into the deed delivered at Settlement and shall not survive Settlement except as provided in Paragraphs 7, if any, and E; that unless amended in writing, it contains the final agreement between the parties hereto, and that they shall not be bound by any terms, conditions, oral statements, warranties or representations not herein contained; and that it shall be construed under the laws of the Commonwealth of Virginia.

## CONTRACTS: OBSERVATIONS AND PROCEDURES

In most transactions, the real estate licensee helps the parties to fill in and execute the sales contract; it is only later that an attorney is consulted. The fact that a standard form (which normally has been approved by attorneys) is used does not excuse the licensee from pointing out to both parties the fact that the contract is a legally binding document and that legal advice should be sought if either party has legal questions. It is possible for either party to make the agreement contingent upon review and approval by an attorney.

If anyone who is party to a real estate sales contract cannot be present at the closing and must be represented by an attorney-in-fact, the licensee should be aware that in Virginia the power of attorney must specify the transaction as well as the parties involved; a general power of attorney will not suffice. The lender in such a case frequently requires an "alive-and-well statement" or similar certification showing that the person granting the power of attorney was in good health at the time of the signing of the deed. The power of attorney must be notarized and be recorded with the deed. The use of military notaries public must be discouraged, since many such persons are from outside Virginia and do not comply with Virginia Code in notarizing or drawing up documents.

Ideally, the status of the seller's title should be known before any contract of sale is signed; in practice, this is rarely the case. The seller may not know the status of his title or the extent of his ownership. If the seller contracts to convey a greater interest than he actually owns, the buyer may obtain (by suit for specific performance) as much title as the seller owns, with a reduction in the purchase price for the deficiency. If the seller acted in good faith, the buyer may be entitled only to nominal damages.

The licensee should determine the age, mental competency and marital status of the seller; a person under age 18 may not convey real property in Virginia, nor may a person judged by the court to be mentally incompetent. Except for a person who owns "a sole and separate equitable estate" (*femme sole* or *homme sole*), the seller's spouse must join in the contract so that the curtesy or dower interest is conveyed. If one spouse or both spouses do not sign, the courts will not order specific performance on the contract unless the buyer is willing to accept a deed that remains subject to the dower or curtesy interest; no reduction in price would be ordered, either. The buyer may still sue the seller for breach of contract, since the seller could not convey the property with a clear title.

The capacity in which each signer executes the contract should be clearly stated, whether the signer is an individual, a married couple, a partnership, a corporation or any other legal entity.

Property descriptions on sales contracts need not be as detailed as those on deeds; ordinarily, a residential description that includes the lot and block numbers and plat designation as well as the city and state is sufficient. For sales of land involving acreage, the seller frequently prefers to sell the land *in gross*. The number of acres will be modified by "approximately" or "more or less" so that no later adjustment in the purchase price will be required.

While the contract implies that all improvements and appurtenances to the land will convey, it is best to specify any matters where doubt could arise. Even if a phrase such as "and all improvements thereon" is included, it would remove ambiguity to specify whether a fence is or is not on the property, for example.

In contracts involving construction between contract signing and closing, the ownership of the improvements being constructed is important. Plans and specifications should be incorporated into the contract. Any changes that arise during the course of construction must be acknowledged by all parties in writing; needless to say, the original plans should be as detailed as possible.

The sales contract should address questions of personal property and fixtures involved in the transactions. Particularly vexing are items that are neither obviously personal property (such as clothing) nor obviously fixtures (such as the toilet); disposition of items like appliances, window treatments, lawn statuary, portable sheds, television antennae, etc. generally cause far more trouble than their monetary worth if not addressed in the contract.

In contracts calling for the buyer to assume the seller's existing deed of trust, the licensee must make sure that the note can be assumed; most conventional notes now cannot be assumed. Even when the note can be assumed (as on VA and FHA financing), the seller should be informed that he will continue to be liable on the note (since his name appears as the maker) unless the lender executes a release of the liability, in effect accomplishing a novation of the parties to the note. Such releases are granted only in unusual circumstances.

The financing of the purchase must be clearly specified in the contract. The disposition of the earnest money (to closing costs or purchase price), additional down payment at settlement and amount of loans to be assumed or obtained should be given. Frequently the buyer wishes to limit liability in the event of rising interest rates and may specify the upper limit of the interest rate and the term of the loan to be obtained. The contract should clearly state whether any of the conditions in the contract (such as a time limit for obtaining a loan commitment), if not met, would void the contract or whether either party may terminate the agreement upon giving specified notice.

The licensee must make the buyer aware that under Virginia law, a sale of used property does not imply a warranty by the seller as to the home's condition. Many defects may be hidden; a qualified inspector may be the buyer's most reliable means of ascertaining the true condition of the property. Should the buyer learn through an inspection by a qualified inspector of defects in the physical condition of the property, he should have the option to terminate the contract. On the other hand, the seller should have the option to limit (within reason) the time allocated the buyer to make the inspection (e.g., "within ten business days of the signing of this contract") as well as financial liability for repairs. A wide range for negotiations exists in this area of the contract.

Any sales contract that is part of an option agreement must contain all of the conditions of sale, since the option, if exercised, becomes a mutually binding contract.

All parties to a sales contract are subject to an implied condition of good faith. For example, if a buyer does not apply for a loan in a timely manner, he cannot rely on this failure to seek the loan as an excuse to terminate the contract.

The buyer under a real estate sales contract expects to receive marketable title to the property from the seller. "Marketable title" and "insurable title" are not necessarily the same because a title insurance policy may list exceptions against which it does not insure. The seller normally provides that the title conveyed will be subject to easements and restrictive covenants "of record." The buyer will want to ascertain that such encumbrances do not prevent the intended use of the property.

The possession date in the contract is normally the settlement date; if not, a possession agreement should be included as an addendum to the contract (buyer's possession agreement for early possession, seller's possession agreement for possession after closing).

If the settlement date is important, a "time is of the essence" clause may be used; however, it is best in such cases to include contingencies for noncompliance, since such a clause by itself could void the contract if the condition cannot be met. A typical contingency might read, "In the event the closing is not held on the specified date, the party responsible for the delay shall pay the other party to the contract $500 per day until settlement." A modified time-is-of-the-essence clause is found in some contracts: "If the closing is delayed more than 30 days, the seller may, at his option, declare the contract null and void." The language of most sales contracts is quite flexible concerning closing dates; a typical wording is "Settlement shall be . . . on or before (date) or as soon thereafter as title is cleared and papers prepared."

When the buyer and seller have executed (signed) the sales contract, the buyer's interest is called equitable title and gives an insurable interest in the property. Virginia law places the risk of damage to the property during this period on the buyer in the absence of an agreement of the contrary. Most sales contracts in Virginia provide that any such risk of loss is borne by the seller; however, the buyer must verify this. The buyer's equitable title interest is considered <u>real property</u>; thus, if the seller dies before closing, his heirs have only a personal property interest in the land and will receive the purchase price at closing. If the buyer dies before closing, his executor or personal representative will be required to pay the purchase price to the seller from the estate.

The buyer may assign his rights under a contract unless the contract forbids it; under such an assignment, the seller must convey to the assignee. However, unless the seller agrees otherwise, the original buyer remains liable for payment. The licensee must exercise special care when dealing with a contract in which the buyer is listed as "Mr. X and/or assigns." Courts have held that, if an assignment takes place and the assignee goes bankrupt or is otherwise unable to perform, the person acting as agent who permitted or advised in favor of the assignment may be liable for malpractice.

## REPRESENTATIONS AND WARRANTIES

The rule of *caveat emptor* (let the buyer beware) is still a principle of law regarding used houses. If the buyer discovers after closing any physical defects in the property, he must bear the loss unless the seller has warranted the property or committed fraud (active misrepresentation or concealment, including words or acts that would throw the buyer off guard).

From the seller's viewpoint, it is best to disclaim all representations or warranties ("as is"). The buyer will normally wish an inspection to verify the condition of the property. A more evenhanded approach would be for the seller to warrant specific improvements. In many areas it is customary for the seller to warrant the heating, plumbing, electrical and air-conditioning systems and equipment to be in working order at the time of settlement; the buyer is frequently given the opportunity for a "walk-through" inspection to verify that these items are in working order and that no material changes (storm damage, vandalism, etc.) have occurred since the signing of the sales contract. If any such changes occur, the seller is required to inform the buyer of them regardless of whether a walk-through inspection is to be performed.

For new homes, the builder normally supplies a detailed warranty list, primarily for the purpose of limiting liability. At the time of settlement, there is an implied warranty that the dwelling and its fixtures (to the best actual knowledge of the seller) are free from "structural defects" and constructed in a workmanlike manner. A structural defect is one that reduces the stability or safety of the structure below accepted standards or restricts the normal use of the structure. The implied warranties continue for one year after the date of transfer of title or the buyer's taking possession, whichever occurs first.

## QUESTIONS

1.   How are records of real estate transactions handled in Virginia?

   a.   The salesperson keeps the records for three years.
   b.   The closing attorney keeps original documents, with copies for the broker.
   c.   The broker maintains the records at the main place of business or a designated branch office.
   d.   The records must be filed with the REB within 90 days of closing and maintained there for five years.

2.   Which of the following categories of funds would not be kept in the broker's trust or escrow account?

   a.   Earnest money deposits and down payments
   b.   Rental payments and security deposits
   c.   License renewal fees paid by the broker's sales associates.
   d.   Money advanced by the broker's principal

3.   In the normal sales contract, which of the following are permissible uses for the earnest money?

   a.   To apply to closing costs at settlement
   b.   To pay for appraisal fees at loan application
   c.   Hazard insurance binder
   d.   All of the above

4.   Once placed in the escrow account, the earnest money may be withdrawn for any of the following reasons, except:

   a.   The transaction has been consummated.
   b.   A court of competent jurisdiction orders disbursement.
   c.   The buyer demands the money back as forfeit damages.
   d.   The broker, at termination, pays the money to the party entitled to receive it, according to the contract.

5.    When can earnest money be paid as commission prior to closing?

    a.    When agreed by buyer, seller and broker(s)
    b.    Under no circumstances
    c.    The portion due the broker may be withdrawn at any time.
    d.    When a promissory note is deposited instead

6.    Commingling of funds is involved in which of the following?

    a.    Broker has one checking account into which all monies are deposited, including earnest money deposits.
    b.    Broker buys 90-day certificate of deposit, notifying buyer.
    c.    Broker pledges certificate of deposit (bought with earnest money deposit) as security for a loan.
    d.    All of the above

7.    Jared Grogan, salesman for Hilgard Realty, negotiates a sales contract for his client, Mr. Swalls, who listed the home with Hilgard Realty five months ago.  The market is unstable; the buyer, Mr. Keys, requested a reply to his offer "as soon as possible" to avoid rate changes.  The offer was presented and signed on Tuesday.  Due to a busy schedule, salesman Grogan forgot to get the signed contract to Mr. Keys on Wednesday; remembering it Thursday morning, he got it to Mr. Keys by noon.  Unfortunately, interest rates rose 1 percent Thursday morning, disqualifying Mr. Keys for the loan.  Is Grogan at fault here?

    a.    Yes; timely delivery could have permitted Mr. Keys to "lock in" an interest rate he could afford.
    b.    No; nothing could prevent the rate change.
    c.    No; his response was "as soon as possible" considering his busy schedule.
    d.    No; Mr. Keys should have applied for the loan regardless of whether his offer had been accepted.

8.    May an offer be presented to the seller if he has already accepted another offer?

    a.    Yes, but the new offer must be treated as a "backup."
    b.    Yes; if the new offer is better than the old one, it may replace it.
    c.    No; once a property is under contract, no new offers can be presented.
    d.    Only if the new offer is received within 48 hours of acceptance of the first one (first right of refusal).

9.    A tree falls on the seller's house a week before settlement.  Who must be informed?

    a.    Only the hazard insurance company
    b.    No one; the risk is the buyer's (caveat emptor).
    c.    The seller's attorney
    d.    The buyer, both brokers and the seller's insurance company

10. The buyer, Mr. Dorf, and the seller, Mrs. Kling, had trouble negotiating because the local area's FHA loan ceiling was only $80,000, and both Dorf and Kling agreed that the house was worth $95,000. They finally agreed on an $85,000 sales price, with $5,000 down payment and an $80,000 FHA loan, and a secret $10,000 orally promised to be paid to Mrs. Kling. Seven percent of the $10,000 as well as of the $85,000 was to go to Hal Willton, the broker who negotiated the transaction. Which of the following would be true of his situation?

    a. The $10,000 promised to Mrs. Kling is unenforceable.
    b. The FHA loan could be foreclosed.
    c. The broker's license could be revoked.
    d. All of the above

11. Salesman Jake Scoggins has persuaded buyer Myra Oxman to make an offer on his listing at 27 Evans Street. To his surprise, the earnest money deposit was a diamond ring, said by Ms. Oxman to be worth $2,100. What must Scoggins do next?

    a. Refuse the offer till Ms. Oxman writes a check.
    b. Note the diamond ring on the face of the contract.
    c. Place the diamond ring in his safe-deposit box.
    d. Simply write $2,100 in the earnest money blank.

12. According to Virginia's Statute of Frauds, an oral contract for the conveyance of real estate is:

    a. void.
    b. unenforceable.
    c. illegal.
    d. voidable.

13. Mrs. Hannah Speckles has a general power of attorney from her husband, Bill, and comes to the closing where her home is to be conveyed to Mr. and Mrs. Bollman. Is Mrs. Speckles' document sufficient to pass title with her husband unable to be present because of Navy duty in the Mediterranean?

    a. Yes; a general power of attorney can be used to fulfill any legal function, including selling property.
    b. Yes; the general power of attorney is designed for cases in which the seller does not know who the buyer will be at the time the power of attorney is drawn up.
    c. No; the general power of attorney is insufficient unless re-notarized in the presence of the buyer.
    d. No; Mrs. Speckles needs a specific power of attorney, naming the transaction as well as the parties involved.

14.   Which of the following statements is true concerning the equitable title the buyer has between the time the sales contract is signed and the time of closing?

    a.   The buyer's interest is considered real property.
    b.   If the buyer dies before closing, his heirs or estate must complete the transaction and pay for the property.
    c.   State law places the risk of damage to the property being purchased on the buyer unless the contract says otherwise.
    d.   All of the above


15.   Dan Aufweise, a salesperson for Grainger Realty, negotiated a sale in which the buyer, Hercule Poiret, assigned the contract to Vernon Gamble.  Before the closing, Gamble declared bankruptcy and was unable to perform the contract.  Is agent Aufweise liable?

    a.   Yes, he may be sued for malpractice for permitting the assignment.
    b.   No, only Gamble is liable for entering a transaction when he knew he might be unable to complete it.
    c.   No one is liable, since the seller signed the sales contract willingly.
    d.   Only the original party to the contract, buyer Poiret, is liable for making a faulty assignment.

## ANSWERS

1.   c.

2.   c.

3.   a.   Earnest money may not be used for appraisal fees or insurance costs unless agreed by all parties in writing.

4.   c.   The buyer may not forfeit the contract. Only the seller may do so but seldom does (since the buyer still has equitable title and may prevent seller from selling to anyone else until the earnest money has been returned to buyer).

5.   a.

6.   d.

7.   a.

8.   a.

9.   d.   By law, all interested parties must be informed of any material change to the transaction. While answer b is correct in that the risk of damage is (by law) the buyer's unless the contract states otherwise, most sales contracts in Virginia do place the risk on the seller until closing.

10.   d.   FHA loans do not permit secondary financing till after closing. Virginia law forbids secret agreements that conceal the full purchase price from the lender. The secret and oral agreement concerning the $10,000 runs afoul of both statute of frauds and the parol evidence rule. The broker's assistance in this transaction is illegal.

11.   b.

12.   b.

13.   d.

14.   d.

15.   a.

# 12

# Transfer of Title

This chapter deals with the subject of deeds and other instruments conveying title to real property. It considers various modes and forms of conveyances; validity and requisites, such as competent parties, forming contents, consideration, description of parties and property, execution, delivery and acceptance; and the operation, effect and construction of instruments.

## REQUIREMENTS FOR VALID CONVEYANCE

### Grantor

The grantor in the deed must be legally competent to execute the conveyance, and the grantee, to receive the land under the deed. In Virginia, the same person may be the grantor and grantee in a deed. For example, a husband and wife can join in a deed conveying land to husband or wife. The test of legal capacity is the party's mental ability to understand the nature and consequences of that transaction at the time of entering into it. It is presumed that the grantor was competent at the same time of execution of the deed, and the burden of proving incompetence is on the one attacking the validity of the deed.

In Virginia, a minor's conveyance of land is a valid transfer of title to the property, unless it is repudiated by the minor after attaining majority. Such repudiation may occur even though the grantee has already conveyed the property to another purchaser without notice that a minor was the grantor in the previous transaction. In other words, transfers of property by minors are voidable at the election of the minor upon attaining majority.

### Partnership

Legal title to real estate acquired in the partnership name can be conveyed only in the partnership name. The conveyance by a partner in his own name will, however, convey the equitable interest of the partnership if the act is within the authority of the partner. Spouses need not joint in a conveyance of partnership property. The authority of an individual partner to convey on behalf of the partnership must be established.

### Corporation

Corporate deeds should be signed by the president (or acting president, any vice president or other person authorized by the board of directors) and acknowledged. The corporate seal and attestation by the corporate secretary are no longer required. Stockholders can validate acts outside the authority of the corporation. If the corporation has changed its name or is a successor to another corporation, this should be stated in the deed.

## Grantee

A deed to a nonexistent person is a valid conveyance to the intended but misnamed grantee, if the intended grantee exists and if the intention of the parties can be ascertained. The full names of the grantees should be used in preparing the deed.

## Consideration

The practice in Virginia is to recite in the deed that the consideration is "$10.00 and other valuable consideration." Upon recordation, the clerk may write the actual amount of consideration in the top right corner of the first page of the deed in connection with determining recording taxes. The exact consideration paid need not be shown on a warranty deed or quitclaim deed. *Deeds from fiduciaries,* however, should show "love and affection for grantee" or such other language to make it clear that the conveyance is a gift. *Deeds of trust* should indicate the total loan amount and a description of the debt, including the maturity date.

Inadequate consideration alone is not grounds for invalidating the conveyance, through evidence of such inadequacy may be relevant to the issue of fraud or undue influence on the grantor. To invalidate a deed, the inadequacy must be so great as to shock the conscience, and it may arise where an inequality exists in the position or intelligence of the parties.

## Granting Clause

The granting clause states the interest granted and any limitations. Operative words demonstrating the intent to transfer the property (not mere acts of the parties) are absolutely essential to the conveyance of title. Generally the words "grant," "bargain and sell" or "convey" must be used to evidence the conveyance.

## Habendum Clause

This clause is rarely used in Virginia.

## Description of Real Estate

To be effective as evidence of title, the deed must give a description of the real property intended to be conveyed, either in its own terms or by reference to other instruments. If it does not, the deed may be considered void. It is presumed that all property not included in the description is excluded from it. A deed will not be declared void for uncertainty of description if it is possible to ascertain from the description, aided by outside evidence, what property is intended to be conveyed. If there is any doubt which land is to be conveyed, the real estate licensee should request that the closing attorney verify the completeness of the description and its exact correspondence to that contained in the deed to the grantor.

## Exceptions and Reservations ("Subject To" Clauses)

An exception by a grantor is a withholding of title to part of the property described in the deed. If the grantor declares in the deed that he does not grant part of the property being conveyed, he *excepts* that particular part from the conveyance. The exception may be effected by the use of any words expressing the grantor's intent. A similar operation would be for the grantor to *reserve* or retain some right, title or interest in the property, which except for the reservation would pass to the grantee. For a valid exception, the property excepted must be described with as much particularity as required in the description of the property conveyed. Exceptions and reservations can take the form of, among others, reservations of: (1) life estates, (2) property previously sold to another, (3) alleyways or roadways, (4) a vendor's lien or (5) reservations for support and maintenance.

## Signature

A deed should be signed only by the grantor; however, the grantee should also sign if the deed is one of assumption. If a corporate officer executes a deed conveying corporate property, the real estate licensee or closing attorney should have a certified copy of the board of directors' resolution authorizing the conveyance. In addition, partnership documents should be reviewed to determine the necessary signatures when a partnership property is conveyed. The signature of the grantor or grantors is indispensable to the validity of the deed. Where a deed is not signed by one of the grantors, the deed is without effect so far as that grantor is concerned, even though the grantor may have acknowledged the deed. The real estate licensee should inspect the deed at the closing to verify that signatures and acknowledgments are present. The grantor's signature should be exactly the same as shown in the body of the deed.

## Power of Attorney

If a seller or buyer is unable to attend the closing, there are essentially two options: (1) prepare all papers to be signed in advance of the ceremony or (2) use a power of attorney. If a power of attorney is used, it must be signed by the seller with the same formality as a deed. The power of attorney can be general or specific, but a specific power of attorney is required to convey real property in Virginia. In reviewing a power of attorney, the licensee should have an attorney verify that it specifically authorizes performance of all necessary acts, and that the attorney-in-fact performs in accordance with the authority granted in the power of attorney.

It is important to note that *affidavits* and other *sworn statements* cannot be signed by the attorney-in-fact; these *must* be signed by the seller prior to the closing ceremony. The deed or other instrument to be signed must indicate that it is being signed by an attorney-in-fact. Normally this is accomplished by a recital in the body of the instrument or under the signature line.

The purchaser/borrower can also act by and through an attorney-in-fact; but if an institutional lender is making a new loan, the lender's permission should be obtained. The lender may not permit the use of an attorney-in-fact, especially if the loan is subject to truth-in-lending requirements.

A power of attorney must be recorded, and the recording fees are charged to the party using the attorney-in-fact. If the power of attorney is not recorded, it is as though the deed were *unsigned* by the party represented by the attorney-in-fact.

## Acknowledgments

Acknowledgment is necessary for court recordation of the deed or other documents in Virginia, but it is not necessary to pass title. A deed is acknowledged when a notary public signs a certificate stating *either* that the notary public witnessed the actual signing of thedocument, *or* that the person signing has presented the document to the notary and stated that the signature affixed to the document is the signor's signature. The object of the Virginia statute is that the notary must know and certify that the person whose name is signed to the instrument is the person who acknowledged it. A notary public certification that a deed was "subscribed and sworn to" by a grantor satisfies the acknowledgment requirement of the Virginia statute. A clerk of court may refuse any document for recording where the signatures of the parties have not been acknowledged. A party to a deed, if he himself is a notary public or other officer, cannot take his own acknowledgment before himself in his official character. The notary's signature should be checked to see that notary's authorization has not expired and that his name has not changed since he was commissioned.

Whenever possible, if active military personnel are involved in a transaction, it is wise to try to use a *civilian* notary public, since there are specific requirements in Virginia regarding acknowledgments taken before commissioned officers in the military service. Although substantial compliance is all that is required, the documenst may be refused for recordation due to an improper acknowledgment.

## Delivery and Acceptance

Delivery is the transfer of a deed, within the grantor's lifetime, to the grantee or someone acting on the grantee's behalf, in such a manner that the grantor may not rescind the transaction. Delivery is the final act, the formal declaration of the grantor's determination to complete the conveyance. It is an indispensable requisite to the validity of a deed. *Mutual intent* to pass title and ownership from grantor to grantee is necessary; while the deed is still within the grantor's control or subject to his authority, there is no delivery. When the grantor has parted with all control over the deed, delivery is complete, even if made to a third person acting on the grantee's behalf.

Delivery may be inferred by the circumstances surrounding the transaction. Acknowledgment, recording and possession by the grantee of the deed are all circumstances used in determining whether delivery has taken place. The acceptance of the deed is presumed from its delivery unless the grantee rejects or renounces it. Where a grantee accepts a deed and enters into possession under it, the grantee becomes liable to perform any promise or undertaking imposed upon the grantee in the transaction.

## TYPES OF DEEDS

### General Warranty Deed

A covenant by a grantor "that he will warrant generally the property hereby conveyed" is an agreement that the grantor and his heirs or personal representatives will warrant and defend the property forever on behalf of the grantee and his heirs and representatives, against claims or demands of *all persons*. Most sellers convey by general warranty deed.

## Special Warranty Deed

A covenant that the grantor "will warrant specially the property hereby conveyed" is an agreement that the grantor (and heirs, etc.) will defend the property forever on behalf of the grantee (and heirs, etc.) against claims or demands arising by or through the *grantor only*.

The contract should specify the type of deed to be used; if the contract is silent, a general warranty deed should be used. If a grantor wishes to limit his liability, he must require that the deed contain a covenant of special warranty; if the grantor merely conveys "with warranty," the deed is construed as a general warranty deed.

## English Covenants of Title

Generally, the terms "general warranty" or "special warranty" are followed by the phrase "with English covenants of title." In brief, these covenants express the following:

1.  Covenant of "right to convey." This covenant warrants that the grantor has the right, power and authority to convey the land and improvements as well as privileges and appurtenances belonging to the land. The covenant will be broken, if at all, upon delivery of the deed--it does not run with the land--and the grantee has the right of immediate action against the grantor.

2.  Covenant for "quiet possession." The grantor's covenant "that the grantee shall have quiet possession of the land" is an agreement that the grantee (and heirs, etc.) might peaceably enter, possess and enjoy the land (and improvements, etc.). This covenant, which runs with the land, is broken by eviction or obstructed or disturbed possession and *not* by the existence of liens, private easements or unassigned dower. This covenant may be restricted by a special warranty appearing in the same sentence.

3.  Covenant against encumbrances. This covenant warrants that debts and liens against the property have been discharged; it is broken upon delivery of the deed by the existence of liens, building restrictions, private easements or unassigned dower. The covenant does not depend upon the extent of decrease in value but upon burdens, claims or rights that prevent the grantee from acquiring complete dominion over the land.

4.  Covenant for "further assurances." The grantor's covenant "that he will execute such further assurances on the land as may be requisite" is an agreement that the grantor (and heirs, etc.) will, upon reasonable request of the grantee (and heirs, etc.), execute any deeds or instruments to convey absolutely the property to the grantee.

5.  Covenant of "no act to encumber." This covenant is an agreement that the grantor had not executed any deed or other instrument whereby the land will be charged or encumbered.

## Bargain and Sale Deed

A bargain and sale deed is a deed of conveyance that does not contain warranties. In Virginia, usually a deed may be called a Deed of Bargain and Sale, but the granting clause may contain language creating either general warranty or a special warranty.

## Deed of Trust

See Chapter 15.

## TRANSFER TAXES AND FEES

## State, City or County Recordation Tax

With certain exceptions, all deeds are subject to state and city or county recording tax. The state tax is currently 15 cents per $100 (or a fraction thereof) of the consideration paid or of the value of the property, whichever is greater. The county or city tax is currently one-third of the amount collectable by the state, or five cents per $100 (or a fraction thereof). The taxes are usually paid by the buyer and collected at closing. Payment of these taxes is a prerequisite to having the deed recorded.

## Grantor Tax

In addition to the recordation taxes, all deeds are subject to a grantor's tax of 50 cents per $500 (or a fraction thereof) of the purchase price or the value of the grantor's equity in the property. The grantor's tax is paid by the seller and is collected by the clerk of the county where it was recorded.

## Tax on Deeds of Trust and Mortgages

Unless exempted, deeds of trust and mortgages are taxed on a sliding scale according to the amount of the obligation that the instrument secures. If the amount is not ascertainable, the tax is based on the fair market value of the property including the value of any improvements as of the date of the deed of trust. Deeds of trust are subject to city or county recordation taxes, clerk's fees and plat recordation fee, if any.

Deeds of trust securing both construction loans and permanent loans are normally subject to tax on deeds of trust.

## Transfer Fee

For each document admitted to record, the clerk of court will collect a transfer fee of $1, generally paid by the buyer.

### Clerk Fee

In addition to the transfer fee, the clerk of court will collect from the buyer a fee of at least $10 for up to the first three and one-half pages and $1 for each additional page. There are recording fees for plats, certificates of satisfaction and release of judgments. Powers of attorney generally are recorded for a fee of $10.

## ADVERSE POSSESSION

To establish title to land by adverse possession it is necessary to show actual, hostile, exclusive, visible and continuous possession of property for the statutory period of 15 years. The terms "claim of right," "claim of title" and "claim of ownership" mean the *intention* of the adverse possessor to take the land and possess and use it as his own. The terms do not imply any claim of *actual title* or right. Thus "color of title," though it may be relevant in a particular case, is not a requirement for proof of adverse possession in Virginia. The possession of the defendant must be *actual*; more than just a sporadic taking of timber or other products is required. The adverse possession must be *exclusive* to constitute an ouster of the true owner.

When several persons enter upon land in succession, these possessions cannot be "tacked" to preserve the essential continuity unless there is a "privity of estate" between them. In other words, the intent to establish a continuous succession of adverse possessors must be proven. And one cannot sustain the defense of adverse possession if, during the required time period, the possession has been abandoned by the claimant. The occupancy necessary to support a claim of title of adverse possession must be hostile and not by permission.

## TRANSFER OF A DECEASED PERSON'S PROPERTY

When any person with title to real estate that may be inherited dies testate (with a will), the real estate will pass in the following course: Circuit courts serve as probate courts in Virginia. Normally there is a probate section in the clerk's office where wills, lists of heirs, affidavits and other documents related to probate are located. As with other documents, a "will index" is located in the circuit courts. Virginia statutes provide for a proceeding to contest a will's validity.

Until probate the will is only the legal declaration of a person's intent as to such disposition. A will may be revoked at any time after execution, while a deed cannot be revoked after it has been delivered to the grantee. The rule of construction in determining whether an instrument is a will or a contract is that if it passes a present interest, it is a deed or contract; but if it does not pass an interest or right until the death of the maker, it is a testamentary paper. Under Virginia law, a decedent's personal property passes according to the law of the state where the decedent was *domiciled* at death, but the real estate passes according to the law of the state where it is located. Obviously, a testator can only have one last will and testament. A will may be set aside for fraud, undue influence, force or coercion.

No person of unsound mind or under the age of 18 years is capable of making a valid will. The law only requires testamentary capacity at the time the will is made. This is the controlling factor. Neither sickness nor impaired intellect is sufficient, standing alone, to render a will invalid.

No will is valid unless (1) it is in writing and signed by the testator, or by some other person in the testator's presence and by his direction in such a way as to make it manifest that the name is intended as his signature; or (2) it is *wholly* in the handwriting of the testator, who signs the will and acknowledges it in the presence of at least two competent witnesses, present at the same time. These witnesses must also sign the will in the presence of the testator. In Virginia, the testamentary intent must appear on the face of the paper itself. As indicated above, holographic (handwritten) wills are valid in Virginia.

In representing the purchaser of property from a deceased's estate or in taking a listing of an estate property, it is wise to request a certified copy of the will and determine whether the executor under the will has the power of sale and can sign the deed and effectively transfer title to the purchaser. Where the executor does not have the power of sale or where the decedent died without a will, it is necessary that *all* of the heirs and their spouses execute a deed as grantors conveying the property to the grantee.

## QUESTIONS

1.  Joe Smith, an heir under his father's will, was to have inherited real property; however, his father sold it shortly before death and Joe wants to have the sale rescinded on grounds of his father's incompetence. Can he do so?

    a.  Yes; any such pleading by a close blood relative will hold up in court.
    b.  Yes; the grantor would have had to prove competence in court during his lifetime.
    c.  No; a deed can be invalidated due to incompetence only during the grantor's lifetime.
    d.  No; a person is presumed competent unless a court has ruled otherwise.

2.  In Virginia, conveyance of real property by a minor is:

    a.  void.
    b.  voidable.
    c.  unenforceable.
    d.  valid.

3.  Which of the following would most likely *in*validate a deed?

    a.  Grantee's name misspelled
    b.  Property description consisting only of street address, city and state
    c.  Grossly inadequate consideration
    d.  Grantor's spouse failing to sign the deed

4. Janice owns lots 4, 5 and 6 in Gander Estates. Based on an oral agreement, she conveys by deed lots 4 and 5 to Bill, who had the impression he was getting all three lots. He seeks to add lot 6 to the conveyance, saying "much of the value is lost without it." How does he stand?

    a. He owns nothing, for a deed is invalid if based on an oral contract.
    b. He can rescind the sale on the basis of misrepresentation.
    c. He owns all three lots, as the equities in the case plainly show.
    d. He owns lots 4 and 5; anything not included in the deed is excluded.

5. If the grantor in a deed intends to retain a life estate for himself in the property, where would this be indicated?

    a. Exceptions and reservations
    b. Habendum clause
    c. Recital of consideration
    d. Legal description

6. Affidavits and other sworn statements of the seller can be signed by:

    a. the seller.
    b. the seller's attorney-in-fact.
    c. a judge or justice of the peace.
    d. All of the above

7. What is required for delivery of the deed to have taken place?

    a. It must have been taken to the closing attorney.
    b. The grantor must have relinquished all control over it.
    c. The deed must be signed and acknowledged.
    d. None of the above

8. When a grantor conveys property with a deed in which the wording is "warranty," the deed is construed to be which type?

    a. General warranty
    b. Special warranty
    c. Bargain and sale
    d. Quitclaim

9. Which of the following is *not* a condition required for adverse possession claims to be upheld?

    a. Possession must have been for at least 15 years.
    b. Adverse possession must be intentional.
    c. A claim may be sustained by mere taking of produce from the land.
    d. The owner must not also be using the land claimed.

10.   When a person was living in Virginia at the time of death, how would the distribution of his property be determined?

   a.   Personal property located in North Carolina would be distributed according to Virginia law.
   b.   Real property located in North Carolina would be distributed according to Virginia law.
   c.   Personal property may be distributed according to the will regardless of state law or location.
   d.   Real property located in Virginia may be distributed according to the will regardless of state law.

11.   If an attorney-in-fact signed the deed but the power of attorney was not recorded, what is the status of the deed?

   a.   The deed is valid.
   b.   It is as though the deed had not been signed.
   c.   The deed is voidable.
   d.   The deed is valid as between the parties.

### ANSWERS

1.    d.    Competence need not be proven; the burden of proof is upon the person attacking another's competence.

2.    b.

3.    c.    If the consideration is so inadequate as to "shock the conscience," the deed may be considered void.  A grantee's name can be corrected by a correction deed; the property description in answer b is adequate for most circumstances; and the deed in answer d is valid, but may have a cloud on title.

4.    d.

5.    a.

6.    a.    An attorney-in-fact can sign a deed, but a sworn statement must be signed by the person making it.

7.    b.

8.    a.    In cases of ambiguity a document is construed against the person who prepared or presented it.

9.    c.    The claim must be based on actual possession.

10.    a.    Personal property is distributed according to the law of the state where the decedent was domiciled; real property is distributed according to the law of the state where it is located.

11.    b.

# 13

# Title Records

The scope of this chapter involves a general discussion of title records, title examinations and recognizing and resolving title problems that may be revealed by the examination, as well as obtaining title insurance. The purpose of the chapter is to acquaint the real estate professional with the basic procedures and mechanics of a title examination. While the closing attorney or his staff members ordinarily perform the title examination, the real estate licensee frequently has occasion to verify one or more of the items mentioned below.

## TITLE EXAMINATIONS

Generally, it is best to have the examination performed as early as possible, to allow time for dealing with unexpected complications. In addition, there should always be a title "rundown" immediately prior to recording the documents executed at closing. The rundown insures that no adverse interests were recorded against the property between the date of the preliminary title examination and the date the purchaser's title is recorded.

The real estate professional should furnish the purchaser's attorney (who is usually the closing attorney) with a copy of the contract of sale, information concerning any unreleased deeds of trust (whether they are to be satisfied prior to closing or not), any existing title insurance policies (or "back title letters") and any known unrecorded deeds or other liens or encumbrances on the property. The seller is not required to have marketable title until the time of closing and must be given a reasonable time to cure any defects found before settlement. In any letter to the seller, the buyer's attorney should merely point out any title problems he is aware of. If the settlement date is important, the letter should specify a date and may state that "time is of the essence."

The Virginia Wet Settlement Act requires that the deed of trust and any other documents be recorded within two business days of the date of settlement and that all settlement proceeds be disbursed by the settlement agent within this period. The Wet Settlement Act applies only to transactions involving lender-made purchase-money loans that are secured by a first deed of trust or mortgage on real property containing four or fewer "residential dwelling units."

The records should be examined in light of any unrecorded deed that the seller might possess. On taking the listing, the real estate licensee should ask to examine any of the seller's documents relating to ownership of or liens against the property; the licensee's notes on these matters should be made available to the closing attorney if anything unusual is found. If a document in the chain of title refers to an unrecorded deed or other instrument that is *not* in the possession of the seller, a title insurance company should be consulted about the possibility of "insuring over" the defect, or the purchaser must waive the defect and accept the risk. If either of the parties is unwilling to accept the risk of a potential unrecorded instrument, the closing will fail and the parties will be left to whatever remedies are in the contract.

In a title examination, the prospective seller's "chain of title" is developed by searching through the grantee index backwards in time to some predetermined point in order to establish the source of title for each owner in the chain. Then, for each grantor in the chain of title, the examiner searches the grantor's index from the date the grantor acquired title to the date it was transferred to the next grantor in the chain. This process, called "adversing" the title, is done to determine whether any person not in the seller's direct chain of title might have some adverse claim or interest recorded against the property to be conveyed. Finally, the examiner will search other indices to determine whether there are any unrecorded claims against the property, such as judgment liens, mechanics' liens or tax liens. While the real estate licensee does not perform a title search in the normal course of taking a listing, any hint of a title problem should spur him to do as thorough a search as possible and to alert the parties' attorneys in order to anticipate or forestall future problems.

Title examinations may be classified as full or limited searches. In a full search the seller's title must be established for at least 60 years. A limited search is a title examination that goes back less than 60 years. Limited searches are appropriate for some loan assumptions and second mortgage closings (unless, as is frequently the case, the second mortgagee requires lender's title insurance).

It should be explained to the purchaser that an "insurable" title is not the same as a "marketable" title. A title defect that would make the property unmarketable might be excepted or excluded from coverage under the provisions of the title insurance policy. Should someone later make a claim based upon the exception to coverage, the title insurance would not be liable; rather, the purchaser would be left to defend the claim or resolve the defect with his own resources. The closing attorney must also remember that he or she represents by implication to the purchaser upon closing that title is marketable.

If someone other than the closing attorney performs the title examination, the attorney should review the report as soon as possible after receiving it. Defects that may take time to cure should be addressed promptly so as to avoid a possible delay in closing. If the real estate professional is aware of any matters that may constitute defects in title, he or she should promptly notify the closing attorney. It is often wise to ask the sellers whether any title problems surfaced during their purchase of the property. At a minimum, the title report should reveal the following:  (1) record title holder; (2) legal description of property; (3) existing lenders; (4) other lienholders (mechanics' lienors, judgment lienors, tax liens, etc.); (5) status of taxes; (6) easements, covenants and other restrictions; (7) objections to marketability; (8) other matters affecting title; and (9) requirements for vesting marketable title in the purchaser.


## TITLE INSURANCE


Title insurance, like an attorney's opinion letter, is based upon a careful search of the records. Title insurance protects the insured against actual losses suffered because of defects in the record title, hidden defects not disclosed by the record and the cost of defending title against adverse claims. Hidden defects that would not be discovered by a title examiner's search of the records may include the following:  forgery or other frauds; legal or mental incapacity of the grantor; void, unrecorded or expired power of attorney; insufficient delivery of the deed;

undisclosed heirs born after the will was executed; revoked or subsequently discovered wills; or a void or voidable judgment upon which the grantor's title is dependent. Title insurance comes in two forms: (1) owner's title policy, which insures the interest of the purchaser, and (2) mortgagee (lender's or loan) policy, which insures the interest of the lender.

Title insurance, however, does not protect the owner from all claims against the property but only from those defects covered by the terms of the policy. The purchaser's attorney or closing attorney must carefully read the binder and the policy to ascertain what coverage is actually being provided to the insured. On new loans, institutional lenders normally require a mortgagee policy, with the premium paid by the borrower or purchaser. A purchaser may or may not want an owner's title policy. The purchaser's attorney or closing attorney should advise the purchaser of the availability and benefits of owner's title insurance. In addition, the real estate professional should be familiar with title insurance and advise the owner to obtain owner's title insurance. The premium paid is nominal compared to the potential cost an owner could incur in connection with a suit to quiet title or other litigation regarding a defect in title.

A title examination often will reveal objections to title that cannot or should not be waived by the closing attorney and cannot otherwise be cleared by the closing attorney or the title examiner. Title insurance companies will sometimes waive such objections and "insure over" the objection. When the closing attorney requires title insurance to waive an objection, an additional and unanticipated premium may be involved. While it is not always necessary for the real estate professional to advise the purchaser of this possibility, when a title defect is known the title insurance company should be consulted and the purchaser advised of this possibility. Theoretically, the seller should pay any additional cost since he is responsible for conveying marketable title. However, when a third-party lender is involved, as is most often the case, the borrower will normally pay for the mortgagee title insurance policy, which in fact protects the lender. The closing attorney should also advise the purchaser of the risks involved in accepting title subject to the objections.

## INTEREST AND DEFECTS IN TITLE

The owner of the property to be conveyed as shown in the deed records is known as the record title holder. In most cases the seller named in the sales contract is the holder of record in title. Clearly, if the title examination reveals that someone else is the record title holder, there is a problem. Sometimes the problem is simple, as where the husband signs the sales contract but the record title is also in the wife's name. The closer can easily verify with the agent that wife is also a seller. At other times the problem is not so simple, as when the record title holder is deceased and an heir signs a sales contract. In this case, an estate proceeding may be necessary. In the situation in which the record title holder is deceased and not all the heirs can be located (or it cannot be determined if any heirs still survive), the closing cannot take place until the problem is resolved. A closing involving an estate should raise warning flags for the real estate professional, who should promptly notify the closing attorney of the problem and convey any information that may be helpful in obtaining the signatures of the heirs needed to execute the deed.

The purchaser is entitled to a deed from the person who signed the sales contract, even if that person is not the record title holder, so that the grantee/purchaser may rely upon the warranties, if any, given in the deed from the grantor.

A chain of title is comprised of consecutive terms of ownership; a gap in the chain could be caused by an unrecorded deed, a name change, an unadministered estate, a foreign divorce decree or some other circumstance. Unless the missing link can be reconstructed from reliable sources outside the record, the defect will be fatal to the closing. Errors (such as an erroneous legal description, a misspelled name or an improper execution) in a prior recorded deed in the seller's chain of title must be cured before the closing can proceed. Where possible, these problems can be cured by a correction deed from the same grantor to the same grantee; the correction deed must be recorded. A correction deed may not be used to change a greater estate to a lesser estate, nor can it be used to change the identity of the grantor altogether. It is the responsibility of the seller to locate the parties and then to correct the deed.

The real estate professional should be aware that it is not unusual for a title examiner to "pick up" (discover) an unreleased deed of trust on the property. Most often, this is due to the failure of the lender or the closing attorney to have a certificate of satisfaction or deed of release signed by the beneficiary and recorded in a timely manner. Often, unreleased deeds of trust go unnoticed until the seller attempts to sell the property. With an institutional lender, if the lien is in fact paid off, it is relatively easy to have a certificate of satisfaction executed and recorded prior to closing. On the other hand, if an individual or private lender was involved, these situations can cause delays in the closing, primarily due to the problems associated with locating the individual.

A name variance, as distinguished from a simple misspelling, is a variation between the name by which a record title holder acquired title to the property and the name by which he conveyed the title or some lesser interest. If the interest is in the name of a previous record title holder, the seller should provide an affidavit from the prior owner that the person's name in the two documents is one and the same.

If the property is known to be subject to a lease or if a lease is discovered during a title examination, the closing attorney should advise the parties to inquire as to possession. Depending upon the buyer's purpose in acquiring the property, the lease may or may not constitute a defect. The lender should also be advised of the outstanding possessory rights of any person other than the purchaser/borrower. Because leases are often unrecorded and not in writing, the purchaser should always be advised to inspect physically the property to be conveyed well in advance of closing. A discovery that the premises are occupied by someone other than or in addition to the seller indicates a possible possessory interest in a third party.

Many title examiners routinely object to all recorded easements as defects in title. However, as a practical matter, only those easements that in some way restrict the use of the owner are of any consequence to the prospective buyer. It is important to note that not all such easements are necessary. Nonrestricting easements, such as those granted to utility companies to allow reasonable ingress and egress for purposes of maintaining utility service, need only be reported in the title certificate without further action or notice to the buyer.

Restrictive covenants or other restrictions may be recorded with the deeds or simply noted on the recorded subdivision plat or both. Subdivision restrictions or regulations may not be recorded in every deed; however, restrictions may attach *by implication* to each parcel conveyed from a common developer if there is evidence of a general plan or scheme of development. This general plan or scheme operates as constructive notice of the possible existence of restrictions on use. In many cases there is evidence of a scheme, but no restrictions are recorded in the chain of title to the property or in the subdivision plat. The title examiner may have to search the deeds of the surrounding parcels for restrictions that may be imposed by implication against the property to be conveyed.

Reported mechanics' or materialmen's liens must be treated as adverse claims against the property to be conveyed. The purchaser should require that these liens be paid and satisfied of record or discharged by the filing of a proper bond at or prior to closing. Unreported liens are also of concern to the purchaser, who will take the property subject to all mechanics' and materialmen's liens for work or materials furnished within the last 90 days. For this reason the purchaser should require the seller to provide an affidavit that there had been no improvements performed or materials supplied within the 90 days prior to the date of closing. This affidavit, commonly known as a "90-day letter," is required by all lenders and title insurance companies.

Certain items of personal property or fixtures may be included in the sales contract as part of the property to be transferred with the real estate. Major appliances, carpeting and heating and cooling systems are commonly transferred with the realty and are often subject to an outstanding security interest in favor of the party who sold the seller the equipment. If an examination of the Uniform Commercial code or financing statement index reveals a financing statement describing personalty or fixtures that may be considered part of the realty to be transferred, the closing attorney should require that the secured creditor be paid off or require an affidavit or other proof that the items described in the financing statement are not in fact the same as those being transferred at closing. The title examiner should check the financing statements for each owner of record since January 1, 1966 and should examine any filings found to see if they are still effective and cover the real estate being examined, in which case they should be reported. Although financing statements lapse after a five-year period, they may be renewed by filing a continuation statement, which is not always separately indexed.

The term *access* refers to the right of a property owner to enter upon and depart from his property. Unless otherwise provided in the sales contract, the purchaser is entitled to free and unrestricted access to the property. No lender will make a loan that is to be secured by property without access. A problem of lack of access must be cleared prior to the closing.

Judgments constitute liens against all real property that the defendant owns or subsequently acquires. If it is not certain that the judgment is against the seller, who denies being named in the judgment, an affidavit to this effect may be sufficient to protect the purchaser. Judgments against prior owners of property may remain as valid liens *against the property* despite the fact that the property has been subsequently conveyed. The purchaser must require the seller to satisfy all judgments against the property, for they remain as liens until the limitation period of 20 years expires and are still subject to execution.

## QUESTIONS

1.    When is the seller of real property required to have marketable title?

    a.    At the time the listing is taken
    b.    When a sales contract is signed
    c.    By the time buyer's loan is approved
    d.    At settlement

2.   What is the status of a sales contract if defects are found in the seller's title?

   a.   It is automatically rescinded.
   b.   Seller has a reasonable time to correct defects, so the contract is still in effect.
   c.   Buyer may, at his option, cancel the contract and recover the earnest money.
   d.   Contract is in force, and buyer must close the transaction and accept the transfer as long as the defects are curable.


3.   What is the primary requirement of Virginia's Wet Settlement Act?

   a.   Documents must be recorded and disbursements made within two business days of settlement.
   b.   Documents can be recorded only if funds were disbursed at settlement.
   c.   Recording of documents can occur only with actual notice of disbursement of funds.
   d.   Recording of deeds is not necessary if the deed is a deed of gift (i.e., no money changed hands).


4.   Why must the licensee ask to see all documents the seller has concerning the property at the time of taking the listing?

   a.   To find out about unrecorded deeds
   b.   To verify deed of trust loan numbers and payment status
   c.   To learn of any liens that may not be recorded
   d.   All of the above


5.   A full title search goes back how many years?

   a.   20
   b.   40
   c.   60
   d.   To the origin of the title


6.   Title insurance protects the insured against which of the following?

   a.   Losses suffered because of defects in the record title
   b.   Hidden defects not disclosed by the public record
   c.   The cost of defending the title against adverse claims
   d.   All of the above

7. Jack Berndt signed the sales contract as seller of real property to the buyer, Mary Gale. It later became apparent that Mr. Berndt was not record owner of the property but was merely acting on the owner's behalf. Should Berndt sign the deed to Gale?

   a. No; since he is not the owner, his signature would have no significance.
   b. No; the sales contract is automatically rescinded.
   c. Yes; the grantee could then rely upon the warranties in the deed.
   d. Yes; since the grantor is acting on behalf of the owner, his signature fulfills all the owner's functions.

8. Which of the following changes may *not* be accomplished by using a correction deed?

   a. Change from a fee simple to a life estate.
   b. Correct an erroneous legal description.
   c. Respell a misspelled name.
   d. Get the correct signature on an improperly executed deed.

9. In cases where title must be cleared by having correction deeds signed, who is responsible for locating the parties who must sign?

   a. The buyer
   b. The seller
   c. The closing attorney
   d. The real estate professional

10. Potential title problems such as adverse possession, leasehold possession or recent construction can best be detected by:

    a. searching the public records.
    b. survey.
    c. title insurance
    d. inspecting the property.

## ANSWERS

1.   d.

2.   b.

3.   a.

4.   d.

5.   c.

6.   d.

7.   c.   However, the true owner of the property should sign as well.

8.   a.   A correction deed cannot be used to change from a greater to a lesser estate.

9.   b.   Seller is required to provide clear title.

10.   d.

# Real Estate License Laws

The laws governing licensure and practice of real estate in Virginia are contained in Title 54.1, Chapter 21 of the *Code of Virginia 1950* and its subsections, including revisions and amendments through 1988; as well as the Real Estate Board regulations, the most recent version of which was adopted in March and effective in July of 1987. The definitions of real estate broker and salesperson, the necessity for licensure to perform real estate acts and exemptions from necessity for license have been treated in Chapter 5.

## LICENSING PROCEDURES

### Licenses, Registrations and Renewal Fees

All application fees for licenses and registrations are nonrefundable. Fee amounts are as follows:

SALESPERSON LICENSE:

| | |
|---|---|
| BY EDUCATION AND EXAMINATION (ORIGINAL OR RENEWAL) | $ 30 |
| BY RECIPROCITY | $ 55 |

BROKER LICENSE:

| | |
|---|---|
| BY EDUCATION AND EXAMINATION (ORIGINAL OR RENEWAL) | $ 50 |
| CONCURRENT LICENSES (EACH) | $ 50 |
| BY RECIPROCITY | $ 75 |
| FIRM LICENSE | $ 50 |
| BRANCH OFFICE LICENSE | $ 15 |

| | |
|---|---|
| RENTAL LOCATION AGENT REGISTRATION: | $ 30 |

PROPRIETARY SCHOOLS:

| | |
|---|---|
| ORIGINAL LICENSE | $100 |
| ANNUAL RENEWAL | $ 50 |

It will be noted that for both brokers and salespeople the additional cost where reciprocity is involved is $25.

## Expiration, Renewal and Reinstatement of License

Licenses for firms, brokers and salespeople expire two years from the last day of the month in which they were issued.  Proprietary school licenses expire annually on June 30, and rental location agent registrations expire every two years on June 30.

The REB mails renewal notices to licensees or registrants at their last-known home address. Since the obligation to renew a license rests upon the licensee, he must notify the board of any change of address.  The notice the licensee receives outlines the procedures for renewal.  If the licensee has not renewed within 90 days after expiration, the licensee's firm will be notified by the REB; a further notification will be sent to the firm at 180 days after expiration.  In the event that the licensee has not received the REB's notice and renewal form, his license can still be renewed by sending (with the required fee) a copy of the license or registration.

Late renewals of licenses are permitted, but penalties are charged according to the following table:

| LATE PENALTIES | 31-180 DAYS | 181 DAYS-12 MONTHS |
|---|---|---|
| FIRMS AND BROKERS | $50 | $150 |
| SALESPEOPLE AND RENTAL LOCATION AGENTS | $30 | $90 |

These penalties are due *in addition to* the normal fee; thus an associate broker who renews 200 days after expiration must pay $200 to reinstate his license.

After 12 months, renewal is impossible under any circumstances.  The applicant must apply as a new applicant and meet all educational and examination requirements in effect at the time of application.  Licensees whose licenses have been inactive for three years or longer must also meet the educational requirements in effect at the time they wish to return to active status (that is, to affiliate with a broker and become active in the real estate business).

## Individual License

Paragraph 1.5 of the REB regulations permits the use by a real estate broker of an assumed or fictitious name under which to transact business; however, before a license is issued, the broker must sign and acknowledge a certificate provided by the REB showing the name under which the business is organized and conducted and the addresses of the individual's home and place of business.  The certificate must be attested by the clerk of court of the broker's business jurisdiction (city or county where the business is conducted).

## Partnership, Association or Corporation

Each real estate firm must obtain a real estate license *as a firm* before transacting real estate business.  This license is separate and distinct from the individual broker licenses required of each partner, associate and officer or director of the firm who is active in the brokerage business.  The application for this license must disclose the name under which the firm plans to do business, and the license will be issued to the firm under the specified name.

If the firm is a partnership, it must file a certificate with the REB showing the name, business address and residential address of all partners; the name and style of the firm (style refers to the type of partnership into which the firm is organized); the address of the Virginia office of the firm; how long the firm is to continue to operate; and the percentage or part of the partnership owned by each partner. Changes in the partnership must be evidenced by filing a new certificate with the REB within 30 days after the change goes into effect. Firms operating as associations must follow the same rules, and each person within the association must supply the same information as each partner in a partnership.

Firms operating as corporations must observe the same rules as partnerships or associations, and each officer of the corporation, as well as each member of its board of directors, must supply the same information as a partner in a partnership. REB regulations specify that license applications from corporations will not be considered unless the corporation is authorized to do business in Virginia.

### Concurrent Licenses

While a salesperson may be licensed to only one broker in Virginia, the 1987 REB regulations (par. 1.7) give a principal or associate broker the opportunity to affiliate with and become active in "more than one legal entity," so long as the applicant submits a concurrent license form and written affidavits from each broker with whom he is affiliated. The affidavits must show that the applicant has given written notice of concurrent licensure status to the principal broker of each firm involved.

A supervising broker of a branch office may not be concurrently licensed with more than one broker, because this position requires him to be a full-time on-premises real estate broker.

The regulations (par. 1.8) specify that the REB may appoint any committees necessary to advise it in carrying out its responsibilities.

## ENTRY TO THE REAL ESTATE FIELD

The primary purpose of license laws in real estate in Virginia is to protect the public from incompetence or dishonesty on the part of real estate practitioners and to encourage high professional standards within the industry. To this end, REB regulations require not only that anyone performing real estate acts for others for compensation be licensed, but also that anyone applying for licensure meet certain minimum requirements.

### Qualifications for Licensure

REB regulations require applicants for licensure to have a good reputation for honesty, competence and fair dealing. Applicants must not have been convicted of a felony, a misdemeanor involving moral turpitude or a violation of fair housing laws (a plea of *nolo contendere*, or no contest, is deemed a conviction). If the applicant is licensed in real estate in a jurisdiction outside Virginia, his license must be in good standing; an applicant will not be considered qualified for licensure in Virginia if his out-of-state license was suspended, revoked or subject to any other discipline within five years prior to applying in Virginia.

The applicant must be at least 18 years old and must meet the current Virginia educational requirements *prior to* sitting for the licensing exam. Current requirement for salespeople is a course in the Principles of Real Estate comprising a minimum of 45 classroom hours; the applicant must pass the course with a minimum grade of C or (if the final examination determines the course grade) a final exam score of 75%. Once the coursework is completed, the applicant may sit for the state licensing examination; for salespeople, the passing grade on the exam is currently 79% on the general portion and 82% on the state portion. Both portions must be passed at the same sitting for the applicant to be eligible for licensure; if one section is passed and the other failed, the applicant must retake the entire examination (which is offered once a month).

Once the exam for licensure is passed, the applicant may apply to become an active licensee. Affiliation with a principal broker or designated supervising broker must take place within 12 months of passing the state licensing examination, or the applicant must retake (and pass) the exam. Applicants may also apply directly to the board to have their licenses on inactive status.

Educational requirements for the broker license are 180 classroom hours beyond the Principles of Real Estate; these may be taken as six three-hour courses in the quarter system or four three-hour courses in the semester system, or a state-certified equivalent, with course content in the areas of real estate brokerage, real estate finance, real estate appraisal, real estate law and any additional courses approved and certified by the REB.

Virginia mandates an experience requirement for licensure as a real estate broker: the applicant must have been actively engaged as a real estate salesperson for at least 36 of the 48 months immediately preceding application. "Actively engaged" as used here means that the applicant must have been engaged in real estate activities under the supervision of a real estate broker for an average of at least 20 hours per week. Anyone who has previously held a Virginia broker's license in good standing (i.e., not revoked) at the time of lapse can be reinstated as a real estate broker *without* having to meet the experience requirements (i.e., without being actively engaged as a salesperson for 36 months) by completing the current educational requirements and passing the broker examination.


## Licensure by Reciprocity

An individual who is currently licensed in a jurisdiction outside Virginia may obtain the Virginia real estate license *without* taking the Virginia written examination by meeting the following requirements:

1.   The applicant must be at least 18 years old.

2.   Current licensure (salesperson or broker) must have been achieved by passing a written examination in the original jurisdiction where the license was granted. The examination must be substantially equivalent to the Virginia examination.

3.   The application must include a signed affidavit certifying that the applicant has read and understands the Virginia real estate license law and the REB regulations.

4.   The applicant must be in good standing as a real estate salesperson or broker in any jurisdiction where licensed. The license must not have been suspended, revoked or subject to other discipline in any other jurisdiction in the five years preceding application in Virginia. The applicant must have a *certificate of licensure* sent from the jurisdiction(s) where he or she is now licensed. The certificate must

be current (dated no more than 30 days prior to the date of applying for a Virginia license).  The certificate is not a copy of the out-of-state license; rather, it is a history of the applicant's licensure:  when and where he received his prelicensingeducation, when and were he took the state licensing examination, when and with whom he affiliated in real estate brokerage, any changes in affiliation, as well as any charges brought against him, together with their resolution.

5.  (Salesperson *only*) The applicant must have been actively engaged (as defined above) in real estate for 12 of the 36 months preceding application or must meet educational requirements substantially equivalent to those in Virginia (i.e., must have passed a course in the Principles of Real Estate comprising at least 45 classroom hours).

6.  Like in-state applicants, the out-of-state applicant must have a good reputation for honesty, fair dealing and competence and must not have been convicted of (nor pled *nolo contendere* to) a misdemeanor involving moral turpitude, a felony or a fair housing violation.

7.  (Broker *only*) The applicant must have been *licensed* as a real estate broker and *actively engaged* as a real estate broker or salesperson in the current jurisdiction for at least 36 of the 48 months preceding application in Virginia and must meet educational requirements substantially equivalent to those in Virginia as listed above.

8.  The applicant must submit $20 to the Transaction Recovery Fund.

9.  If not a resident of Virginia, the applicant must submit a completed form consenting to service of process.  This assures that an out-of-state licensee, who is also licensed in Virginia and who commits an offense for which he may be sued, cannot escape the consequences of the suit merely by returning to his home state. The suit will be binding wherever he goes.

## Rental Location Agent

A rental location agent is an individual who solicits listings of properties available for rent and receives fees when the properties are rented through his efforts; and who sells lists of properties available for rental to prospective tenants.  While rental location agents were formerly licensed in Virginia, they are now only registered with the REB.

The rental location agent must also have a good reputation for honesty, fair dealing and competence and must be at least 18 years old.  An individual may *not* be concurrently licensed as a real estate salesperson and registered as a rental location agent; a rental location agent may *not* be concurrently registered with more than one rental location agency.

The rental location agency may be organized in the same way as a real estate brokerage:  sole proprietorship, partnership, association or corporation.  The firm must have a firm registration issued by the REB.  Each agency must be supervised by a supervising rental location agent, designated by the agency and registered with the REB; he has the responsibility of supervising the activities of the agency and all its registrants.

Registrations are issued to the rental location agency, not the individual rental location agent; the supervising rental location agent is responsible for the maintenance of the registrations. When an individual rental location agent terminates employment or association with the agency for any reason, the supervising rental location agent must notify the REB of the termination by returning the registration by certified mail to the board within ten calendar days. Before returning the registration to the board, the supervising rental location agent must indicate the date of termination and must sign registration.

## Standards of Conduct

The REB regulations specify permissible and impermissible conduct in many areas of the real estate business. Items concerning the broker's place of business have been dealt with in Chapter 5, and those concerning records and deposits of funds are treated in Chapter 11. Many of the regulations concerning grounds for disciplinary actions are relevant here; note that many of the following points concern matters of ethics and practice as well as licensure.

An individual or firm may not obtain a license by false or fraudulent representation, such as by having another person take the examination or using false identification.

A licensee may not use "bait and switch" tactics. In its simplest form, this offence consists of offering for sale a property (often in poor condition) that the broker or salesperson knows will not sell, but the advertisement for which will entice prospective purchasers, who on learning the true condition of the offered property may be "switched" to the property (much more expensive) that the broker really intended to sell. The REB regulation (3.5.14) dealing with this subject specifies that the advertisement or offer must clearly state that the property advertised is in limited quantity; further, the licensee must actually have the quantity he advertises to have. This regulation also applies to rental properties and advertisements and to rental location agents as well as real estate licensees.

The principal or supervising broker must keep on file for at least three years after any real estate closing a complete and legible copy of every document material to the transaction: the sales contract, listing, closing statement and any other relevant forms or documents. (While the broker is required to keep such documentation, the salesperson is also urged to do so. There may be times when the salesperson, who has a comparatively small number of files to maintain, may be able to pinpoint the file needed much more quickly than the broker, who may have hundreds or thousands of such files.)

No individual may hold more than one license as a real estate broker or salesperson in Virginia except for the concurrent license permitted to brokers in paragraph 1.7 of the regulations and cited earlier in this chapter.

For some years there was no limit to the number of times a salesperson or broker could take the state licensing examination. Current regulations, however, are strict and explicit: no currently licensed salesperson may sit for the salesperson exam and no currently licensed broker may sit for any real estate licensing exam in Virginia. These provisions exist, at least in part, for the purpose of curbing abuses such as piracy of examination questions (see below).

The licensee may not withhold from the REB or from any of its authorized agents any documents demanded by the board. These documents (including books, records, copies of listings or contracts) may be relevant to any transaction in which the licensee was involved as broker or salesperson.

The same standards of competence, fair dealing and honesty required of new applicants for licensure are expected to be maintained by the licensee. Failure to do so or conviction or pleas of *nolo contendere* to any misdemeanor involving moral turpitude, felony or violation of the fair housing laws will result in disciplinary action by the REB. If found guilty of any such offense, the licensee must notify the REB of the conviction within 30 days or face further disciplinary action.

## Grounds for Disciplinary Action of Rental Location Agents

Rental location agents may not accept a fee for services without giving the person paying the fee a written contract or receipt that specifies the termination date for the service rendered. The maximum period of service is one year. If no rental is obtained, the rental location agent must agree to repay the customer (on request) any amount of the fee in excess of $10; such payment should occur within ten days of the expiration date of the contract. Further, the rental location agent must warrant accuracy of the information given to customers: If the information is inaccurate or obsolete, he must on request repay the full fee within ten days of the delivery of the inaccurate rental information. The rental location agent must verify the availability of any property referred to a prospective tenant within seven working days prior to the referral.

The rental location agent is required to maintain a registry of all lists of rentals provided to customers as well as all advertisements that he publishes or causes to be published. The registry must provide the address of the property listed or advertised, the date of verification of availability and the name, address and telephone number (if any) of the person who offered the property for rent. The rental location agent must keep the registry for at least three years from the date of the lists or publication of the advertisements.

## Advertising by Licensees

The REB mandates certain restrictions on advertising, the purpose of which is to inform the public of the precise status of the licensee and the property or service advertised.

The broker may not permit the false impression that the property is for sale by owner either by adopting a deceptive business name (e.g., FSBO Realty) or by the manner of advertising. The broker must affirmatively and unmistakably indicate that the property is being marketed by a licensed real estate broker; thus he may not advertise by using only a post office box number, telephone number or street address.

A salesperson or associate broker is prohibited from advertising using only his own name; such an advertisement could give the false impression of trading as a real estate *broker*. All advertising must be under the direct supervision of the principal or supervising broker and in the name of the firm, which must appear on all display signs and other advertising in a size equal to or greater than that of the name of the salesperson or broker.

If the salesperson or associate broker is marketing property in which he has an ownership interest, the advertisement must contain notice that he is a real estate licensee but must not indicate or imply that he is operating a real estate brokerage business.

Two primary categories of advertising are treated in the REB regulations: institutional advertising and merchandise or product advertising. Institutional advertising is that in which the firm advertises itself and its service without mentioning any individual licensee or specific property; the service mark of the firm is considered part of its institutional advertising. An example of institutional advertising would be as follows:

FIVE STAR REALTY

TOP RANKING SERVICE

IN ALL AREAS OF REAL ESTATE

As shown above, institutional advertising must state that the service being advertised is real estate brokerage.

For companies operating as part of a franchise (Century 21, Better Homes and Gardens, RE/MAX, etc.), any logo or service mark appearing as part of written noninstitutional advertising (i.e., as product or merchandise advertising) must conspicuously disclose that the firm using the mark is independently owned and operated; this disclosure is *not* required for these advertisements:

1.   FOR SALE and FOR LEASE signs on the premises of the property for sale or lease

2.   Newspaper or other advertisements for a single specific property, provided that the advertisement occupies no more than 28 standard classified-ad lines in the publication

3.   Telephone directory listings; however, the disclosure *is* required for display ads or "in-column informational" or "business card" ads or the equivalent.

In oral noninstitutional advertising, the licensee must disclose the name under which he is licensed; further, except in telephone communication, the licensee must disclose that the licensed brokerage firm or sole proprietorship to which he is licensed, if a franchise, is independently owned and operated.

One of the most troublesome practices found in the real estate industry is the failure to make prompt disclosure of the licensee's status. In calling a "for sale by owner," the licensee must state his registered name, firm affiliation and business *immediately,* so that the homeowner trying to sell may not be misled into believing that the caller is a potential customer. A sample introduction follows:

FSBO:   Hello.
Licensee: Hello, I'm calling about an advertisement for a home for sale. Is this the right number?
FSBO:   Yes, it is.
Licensee: I'm Bryan Spratlow of Garble Realty, and I'm soliciting listings. I wonder if you would like to see what my company and I can do to market your home.

Most homesellers expect to receive calls from real estate companies and do not mind straightforward calls. Deceptive calls, however, are against the law and are poor business practice.

## Investigation by the Board

Upon the complaint of any person, the REB may investigate actions that are alleged to violate the Virginia Code or the REB regulations. The persons whose actions may be investigated include licensees (and rental location agent registrants) as well as anyone who "presumes to act in such capacity." The complaint may include evidence, either by document or by testimony. The board may investigate on its own motion (i.e., without prior complaint) if it sees cause for doing so.

If evidence of a violation by a licensee is found, it normally results in action being taken against the licensee. Action may also be taken against the principal broker with whom the licensee is affiliated if it appears to the satisfaction of the board that the principal broker "knew or should have known" about the violation.

If the board takes action resulting in a principal broker's license being revoked or suspended or renewal denied, such action automatically results in an order that the licenses of all licensees affiliated with or employed by the firm (or sole proprietorship) be returned to the board. The subordinate licensees affected by this action must *immediately* stop listing and selling property. They may then seek another broker with whom to affiliate, and on that broker's written request, the REB will reissue the licensee's license to the new broker. At that point the licensee may re-enter the active phase of the real estate business.

## Schools

Courses in real estate, both in prelicensing instruction (principles) and postlicensing instruction (broker courses, continuing education), may be offered by accredited colleges, universities and community colleges or by accredited proprietary schools.

Instructors for courses in real estate must meet certain minimum standards to be certified by the REB: they must have a baccalaureate degree in real estate (or in business with a major in real estate or a closely related field); *or* a baccalaureate degree in any field combined with two years' experience as an active licensee within the past five years, with no discipline having been exercised against them; *or* seven years (within the past ten) of discipline-free active experience as a licensee with a broker license.

The Principles of Real Estate course must have a written, monitored final examination. In college courses, the final course grade must be at least a C; in any course in which the final examination determines the grade, the final exam score must be at least 75 percent. The school may use any textbook approved by the REB, which furnishes a list of approved texts upon request.

Schools must be held in suitable facilities, with a library available to students outside class hours. Room arrangement should allow for workshops and small groups as well as lectures; a maximum of 50 students in a class is recommended. The school building must meet relevant city codes, including fire safety and sanitation standards. The school's certificate of approval and license must be conspicuously displayed.

## Withdrawal of Approval

The REB may withdraw approval of a school for any of the following reasons: (1) if the school, instructors or courses no longer meet REB's standards; (2) if the school solicits information from anyone in order to discover questions that have been asked on past examinations or that may be asked on future examinations; (3) if the school distributes or communicates examination questions to anyone without prior written consent of the copyright owner to do so; (4) if the school advertises (through an agent or otherwise) in a fraudulent, deceptive or misrepresentative manner; or (5) if officials, instructors or designees of the school sit for a real estate licensing examination for any purpose other than to obtain a license as a broker or salesperson.

It will be noted that points 2, 3, and 5 above directly refer to the integrity of the licensing examination. Practices that were common--even legal--in former years are now strictly forbidden: having students take the test and bring out questions, either memorized or written; using the questions thus compiled to teach subsequent students; or sending teachers to take the test (even sometimes deliberately failing it) in order to examine the test or gain knowledge of test questions. Such practices undermine the professional preparation of the licensee and encourage teaching to the test rather than teaching the subject matter in a thorough, reliable and comprehensive manner.

In addition to the normal course content, the REB has provisionally included fair housing statutes and REB regulations among the subjects to be covered in the Principles of Real Estate; these two new topics will become effective as of January 1, 1991, at which time the course requirement will increase to 60 classroom hours.

## REAL ESTATE BOARD

The REB is under the direction of the Department of Commerce and is headquartered at 3600 W. Broad Street in Richmond. The board has five members, each of whom must be a qualified real estate licensee (salesperson or broker); as a minimum, the licensee must have been active in the field for at least five years preceding service on the board.

Board members serve four-year terms and may succeed themselves once. They are appointed by the governor, with one member chosen each year; thus, board terms are always staggered. In point of fact, the members frequently reflect statewide distribution, with one from the northern Virginia area, one from near Richmond, one from Hampton Roads, one from western Virginia and one from central Virginia. This distribution has no legal basis or necessity but arises from custom. Board members choose their own chairman each year.

The board must enforce the real estate license law. It issues, suspends, revokes or denies renewal of a license; it fines licensees; and it makes rules and regulations to carry out the license law.

The REB administers four additional laws in Virginia: the Transaction Recovery Act, the Condominium Act, the Fair Housing Act and the Time Share Act.

It is not within the purview of the board to regulate commission rates or fee schedules licensees may charge customers or clients; such commissions are fully negotiable between the parties and no maximum is set by law. The board does not adjudicate disputes between or among licensees; such matters may be settled through arbitration by a local Board of Realtors (provided both parties to the dispute are members) or by filing suit in a court of competent jurisdiction.

The board does not establish standard contract forms for listings, sales contracts or leases. While the Virginia Association of Realtors (VAR) frequently has sample forms that may be used, in reality there are no standard forms in Virginia but only local forms with more or less currency depending on the market impact of the local Board of Realtors. The licensee must, therefore, be familiar with the local forms and the meanings of all entries on them before practicing real estate in a new area.

## Hearings of the Board

The REB may investigate *any* person it thinks may have violated license laws. Such investigation may be initiated on someone's complaint (again, *anyone* may file a complaint) or may be undertaken because the board or board member sees reason to investigate; the REB need not wait for a complaint to be filed before investigating. If evidence of a violation is found, the board holds a hearing. The licensee whose acts are being investigated and the principal or supervising broker are notified by certified mail of the charges being investigated, as well as the time and place of the hearing. The licensee may submit evidence on his behalf and may subpoena witnesses.

## Penalties for Violations

If the decision of the board is that the licensee has violated license law, the board has the power to suspend, revoke or deny renewal of the licensee's license. This action is effective ten days after the licensee has been notified of the decision, giving time for the licensee to order business affairs. The board may also fine the licensee or may issue a consent decree, in which the licensee, while not admitting guilt, nonetheless agrees not to commit the offense again and pays a fine.

If the licensee is also found guilty of the offense in a court of law, the offense is treated as a Class III misdemeanor punishable by a fine of up to $1,000. The licensee is also subject to civil liability (i.e., may still be sued in civil court), and any further damages awarded if the judgment goes against him.

## Appeals

If a license is suspended, revoked or denied, the licensee may file an appeal with the clerk of the circuit court having jurisdiction. The licensee must notify the REB of intent to appeal and must file within 30 days of notifying the board of such intent.

## Virginia Condominium Act

In general terms, this act was addressed in Chapter 8; it will suffice here to point out some specific responsibilities of the Real Estate Board in respect to the act.

Once the developer of the condominium has filed the required registration with the REB, the board will review the application. Until the registration is approved, the developer may not accept contracts on the units, only nonbinding reservations. Once the condominium is approved the developer may take binding contracts but must allow the buyer a ten-day rescission period, beginning from the signing date of the contract or from the buyer's receipt of the public offering statement, whichever is later.

## Virginia Real Estate Transaction Recovery Act

This fund was created on July 1, 1977, to protect real property consumers from the improper or dishonest conduct of licensees, including the wrongful taking or conversion of money, property or other things of value, and fraud, willful misrepresentation or deceit. These are *deliberate criminal acts* and do *not* include matters that could be construed as errors or omissions, which are normally covered by errors and omissions insurance usually carried by licensees. Thus the conscientious licensee who makes mistakes unintentionally is not the target of the TRA.

Assessment. Each new licensee must pay a sum into the Transaction Recovery Fund, currently $20. The board may assess from every active licensee a sum sufficient to bring the fund up to its minimum statutory balance, which is $400,000 now. No licensee may be assessed more than $20 in a two-year period. If the licensee does not pay his assessment within 30 days after final notice from the board, his license is automatically suspended.

Recovery from the fund. A person who suffered loss or injury as a result of the deliberate acts of a licensee while the licensee was acting as an agent should proceed first against the licensee in a court of competent jurisdiction. If a judgment is awarded against the licensee and the licensee is unable to pay, the aggrieved party may make a claim in court against the Transaction Recovery Fund. In order to recover, the aggrieved person must meet three conditions:

1. He must file claim within six months after the judgment becomes final. While other judgment enforcements in Virginia may be delayed as long as 20 years, the judgment creditor in a TRF case cannot wait until the licensee is in better financial condition to enforce but must do so within the specified time limit.

2. The creditor must file an affidavit stating that an investigation of the judgment debtor's (i.e., the licensee's) real and personal assets--all that might be available to satisfy the debt--has been made.

3. The creditor must show proof that the assets were insufficient to satisfy the debt. If partial satisfaction was made, the creditor must state the amount paid and the balance still due.

If these conditions are met, the board will pay any remaining deficiency (subject to the limits shown below), not including interest, or punitive damages, but including attorney's fees and court costs. If the assets of the fund are not sufficient to satisfy all claims outstanding against it, the board will pay the claims in the order in which they were submitted.

Recovery from the fund is limited to "real property consumers." Thus real estate licensees may not recover from the fund as an aggrieved party nor may an agent of the licensee or his or her spouse or child. In addition, lenders, contractors and real estate developers may not collect from the fund.

Limitations on recovery. The total of all claims arising from a single transaction may not exceed $50,000; if the claims total more than this, they are prorated. The maximum claim of a single creditor is $20,000. The total of all claims from the improper acts of one licensee is $100,000 per biennial period.

Revocation of license. If a claim is paid from the Transaction Recovery Fund as the result of the actions of a licensee, the licensee's license is revoked *immediately*--there is no ten-day waiting period. The licensee may not apply for a new license until he repays the entire amount paid out from the fund, including annual interest. Bankruptcy does not relieve the licensee from this debt. (Note that bankruptcy is quite probable, given the financial condition already verified in the claim filed by the aggrieved party.)

It has been pointed out that an out-of-state licensee may not be granted a Virginia license if his out-of-state license was the subject of discipline within the past five years. In the case of a Virginia licensee's violation resulting in payment from the Transaction Recovery Fund, the board may enforce a similar five-year period, which may commence when full repayment to the fund by the former licensee has been made. The board may take additional disciplinary action against the licensee after repayment to the fund.

From this discussion it should be clear that payment from the Transaction Recovery Fund takes place only upon a serious criminal violation upon the part of a licensee. If a licensee is guilty of an action that necessitates such a payment, the practice of real estate will not be open to him for some time.

## QUESTIONS

1.    Sally has passed the coursework and the licensing exam in Virginia; her friend Judy is already licensed in another state but is becoming licensed by reciprocity in Virginia. How do the fee amounts for the ladies' licenses compare?

      a.    They are the same.
      b.    Sally's license is $25 less.
      c.    Judy's license is $55 more.
      d.    Judy's license is $180 more.

2.    In Virginia, a real estate salesperson license is in effect for how long?

      a.    12 months
      b.    Two years
      c.    Three years
      d.    Five years

3.   Who must notify the Real Estate Board of a licensee's change of address?

   a.   The licensee
   b.   The post office
   c.   The broker
   d.   The local Board of Realtors

4.   Jason's salesperson license expired on August 31, 1987, but he has failed to renew until March of 1988.  How does he stand now?

   a.   He cannot renew but must reapply as a new licensee.
   b.   He can renew but must pay a penalty fee of $30.
   c.   He can renew but must pay a penalty fee of $50.
   d.   He can renew but must pay a penalty fee of $90.

5.   David Ware, a broker who is a sole proprietor, wishes to do business under the name "Daddy Warebucks Realty."  May he do so?

   a.   No; assumed or fictitious names are illegal in Virginia.
   b.   Yes; he must, however, change his own name legally.
   c.   Yes, as long as he signs and acknowledges a REB certificate to that effect showing his true name.
   d.   Yes; since he is a sole proprietor, he can use whatever name suits his fancy.

6.   Which of the following is not part of the required information to be filed with the REB by a real estate partnership or association?

   a.   Name and style of the firm
   b.   Number of salespeople the firm intends to hire
   c.   Home address of each officer of the firm
   d.   How long the firm is to continue

7.   Under the concurrent licensure provision in Virginia, who may be simultaneously licensed with more than one firm?

   a.   Any licensee
   b.   Any licensed broker
   c.   Any licensed broker other than a supervising broker
   d.   A licensed salesperson *only*

8.   Which of the following is not a requirement for a broker license?

   a.   A college degree
   b.   180 classroom hours in designated broker courses
   c.   Experience of 36 months' active work in real estate within the past four years.
   d.   A good reputation for honesty, fair dealing and competence

9.   A salesperson from another state received her license by virtue of passing a 30-hour
     course in the principles of real estate and passing an exam; she has been active in real
     estate sales for six months.  What must she do to get a Virginia license by reciprocity?

     a.   She needs only to send in her fee.
     b.   She needs only to retake the principles course.
     c.   She needs to take both principles and the state exam.
     d.   She needs only to take the Virginia licensing exam.


10.  Shirley goes to look at a property advertised as an amazing bargain in the newspaper.
     She sees that it is, indeed, "too good to be true."  The salesperson on the site directs her
     to another, better (but more expensive) property down the street.  This offense is
     commonly known as:

     a.   steering.
     b.   bait and switch.
     c.   redlining.
     d.   misrepresentation.


11.  Jacob Grady pays his principles of real estate instructor, Ken Badlow, $1,000 to take the
     Virginia licensing exam for him.  When caught, which of these persons will be subject to
     discipline?

     a.   Both
     b.   Neither
     c.   Grady only; it is his prospective license that is in doubt.
     d.   Badlow only; as a certified instructor, he knew better.


12.  Why is it illegal for a currently licensed salesperson to take the state licensing
     examination for a salesperson?

     a.   To avoid overcrowding at test centers
     b.   To curb abuses such as piracy of examination questions
     c.   To prevent some salespeople from being better prepared than others for the
          broker examination
     d.   To minimize paperwork for the REB


13.  Which of the following names of a real estate brokerage firms would most likely be
     subject to disciplinary action?

     a.   En Garde Realty
     b.   U. B. Ware Realty
     c.   The Homeowner's Real Estate Exchange
     d.   Cut Rate Realty

14. "Doctor Bell's Realty: We Make House Calls!" is what kind of advertising?

   a. Institutional advertising
   b. Noninstitutional advertising
   c. Merchandise advertising
   d. Product advertising

15. In telephone communication with potential clients or customers, how soon must the licensee identify himself and his firm?

   a. Immediately
   b. When asked by the person on the other end
   c. Before the end of the conversation
   d. At a subsequent visit to the prospect's property

16. What is a certificate of licensure?

   a. A copy of the licensee's license
   b. A certified history of one's licensure
   c. A receipt for biennial licensure fees
   d. An affidavit that licensee has read and understands Virginia license law

17. Janet, a South Carolina licensee recently licensed in Virginia, cheated a Virginia customer, who sued her. Driving back to South Carolina to escape the suit will not help because:

   a. Janet signed a form consenting to service of process.
   b. Janet's acts in Virginia are binding in South Carolina.
   c. A Virginia customer must automatically file suit in all states where a licensee is licensed.
   d. South Carolina has reciprocity with Virginia.

18. The Real Estate Board is administered under what branch of state government?

   a. the Attorney General's office
   b. the Bureau of Housing and Land Management
   c. the Governor's Task Force on Housing
   d. the Department of Commerce

19. Which of the following is *not* a necessary qualification for membership on the REB?

   a. A Virginia real estate license
   b. Five years' active service in real estate (minimum)
   c. A Virginia real estate broker's license
   d. None of the above

20.  Which of the following is true of appointment to the REB?

a.  It is for a four-year term.
b.  Appointment is by the governor.
c.  Appointments are staggered, one per year.
d.  All of the above

21.  Which of the following is a duty of the REB?

a.  Adjudicate disputes among licensees.
b.  Administer the Time Share Act.
c.  Regulate commission rates.
d.  Establish and distribute standard contract forms.

22.  Which of the following laws is administered by the REB?

a.  Fair Housing Law
b.  Condominium Act
c.  Real Estate License Law
d.  All of the above

23.  Which of the following persons may be investigated by the REB for violations of Virginia law?

a.  A real estate broker accused of commingling funds
b.  A nonlicensee accused of managing property without a license
c.  Your aunt, accused of refusing to rent to a Native American
d.  All of the above

24.  If a licensee's license has been suspended by the REB for a violation, how long does he have to order his affairs before the suspension becomes effective?

a.  24 hours
b.  10 days
c.  30 days
d.  6 months

25.  The Transaction Recovery Act was enacted to protect real property consumers against:

a.  errors and omissions by licensees.
b.  criminal acts by licensees.
c.  criminal real estate acts by nonlicensees.
d.  land fraud by developers and subdividers.

26.   Which of the following is true of assessments for the Transaction Recovery Fund?

   a.   Each new licensee pays $50 into the fund.
   b.   The current statutory balance of the fund is $1,000,000.
   c.   If the licensee does not pay his assessment within 60 days after final notice from REB, his license is suspended.
   d.   None of the above

27.   If a person has been harmed by the acts of a licensee acting as an agent, what should he or she do?

   a.   File suit in a court of competent jurisdiction.
   b.   File a complaint with REB.
   c.   File a remonstrance with HUD.
   d.   Seek arbitration by the local Board of Realtors.

28.   If an aggrieved consumer wins a money judgment against a licensee, how soon must the consumer file claim against the Transaction Recovery Fund?

   a.   Within 30 days
   b.   Within six months
   c.   Within five years
   d.   Within 20 years

29.   Which of the following persons may *not* file a claim against the Transaction Recovery Fund?

   a.   A real estate licensee involved in the case
   b.   The wife or husband of a real estate licensee involved in the case
   c.   The son or daughter of a real estate licensee involved in the case
   d.   All of the above

30.   What happens to a licensee when payment is made on his account from the Transaction Recovery Fund?

   a.   He is censured by the board.
   b.   His license is suspended and he has ten days to order his affairs.
   c.   Renewal of his license is denied and he has 30 days to appeal.
   d.   His license is immediately revoked.

## ANSWERS

1.  b.  For salesperson license, in-state fees are $30, out-of-state (by reciprocity), $55.

2.  b.

3.  a.

4.  d.  For the first 30 days after expiration, he pays only the renewal fee. From 31 to 180 days after expiration, he would pay the renewal fee plus $30, and from 181 to 364 days he would pay the renewal fee plus $90.

5.  c.

6.  b.

7.  b.  Note that this does not apply in a practical way to the supervising broker of a branch office who is a full-time on-premises real estate broker who supervises only that office and is at the office or within easy access during all regular business hours.

8.  a.

9.  b.  The Principles of Real Estate course required in Virginia consists of at least 45 classroom hours and the experience requirement for reciprocity is 12 months; since the salesperson met neither requirement in the other state, she must meet either the coursework or the experience requirement in Virginia; she need not take the exam.

10. b.  Steering and redlining are fair-housing violations. While bait and switch is, in one sense, misrepresentation, that term is broad and includes many other offenses.

11. a.

12. b.  It is illegal for anyone to bring test questions out from the test or to communicate those questions to anyone.

13. c.  This company name does not make it clear that the company is a real estate brokerage business; further, it implies that it deals with "for sale by owner" properties. The other names shown may be tasteless but are legal.

14.   a.   The ad names the company and tells what it does but does not mention any specific real property or individual salesperson or agent. Noninstitutional advertising is advertising that does mention specifics and includes merchandise advertising (which includes ads for specific properties) and product advertising (which includes not only properties but the broker's services).

15.   a.

16.   b.

17.   a.

18.   d.

19.   c.

20.   d.

21.   b.

22.   d.

23.   d.

24.   b.

25.   b.

26.   d.   A new licensee pays $20; statutory balance is $400,000; and the licensee has 30 days after final notice to pay.

27.   a.

28.   b.

29.   d.

30.   d.

# 15

# Real Estate Financing

This chapter deals primarily with the financing of single-family residential real estate in Virginia. It does not address commercial or more sophisticated transactions, but many of the concepts addressed apply to such transactions.

## PURCHASE CONTRACTS AND FINANCING

A licensed real estate broker or agent who has negotiated a sale and who has the usual broker's interests in the sale may prepare a routine contract for the transaction. This is not considered to be the unauthorized practice of law. Almost all such contracts are prepared by real estate agents and are usually executed (signed) before being examined by an attorney representing either buyer or seller. If a first deed of trust loan is to be obtained, the contract usually is made contingent upon the purchaser obtaining the loan. The real estate professional must be careful in describing the loan in light of the complexity of the loan terms of prevailing loans. The seller may add the provision that the purchaser will apply for the loan promptly and should the purchaser not notify the seller by a certain date that loan approval has been obtained, the contingency shall be deemed waived. Typically, preprinted real estate contracts provide that the purchaser apply for financing within five days of the date of the contract. The contract should specifically state what type of financing is contemplated: cash, assumption, seller financed or institutional (FHA, VA or conventional). Further, the buyer's agent should provide a ceiling on the interest rate of the loan to be obtained, for example, "the interest rate shall not exceed 11%." If this type of phrase is not inserted in a contract, the purchaser will have to go through with the transaction even if the interest rate rises five percent between the date the contract is executed and the date the purchaser locks in the interest rate.

If an existing loan is to remain on the property, the contract should specify whether it will be *assumed* or whether title will be taken *subject to* the existing loan. Occasionally, the seller will take back a purchase-money note and deed of trust, or the purchaser will pay all cash above the amount of the deed of trust assumed. If the contract is silent concerning financing, the purchaser will be expected to produce cash at settlement and financing will not be a contingency in the contract. The real estate professional should make the purchaser aware that it is generally against the law to borrow the down payment and that the lender will want some evidence that the purchaser has at least 5 percent to 10 percent of the amount of the loan in cash. Generally a lender will not make a loan in an amount that exceeds 95 percent of the value of the property.

## INSTITUTIONAL FINANCING

### Conventional Loans

Nearly every type of financial institution makes conventional deed of trust loans. The note and deed of trust give the lender the right upon default by the borrower to accelerate maturity and give the trustee the right to hold a nonjudicial foreclosure--a foreclosure without a court hearing--to determine the propriety of the action. By signing the note and deed of trust, the borrower waives various rights, including the court hearing; if the borrower believes the foreclosure is wrong, he must seek a hearing. Thus it is extremely important that the borrower understand fully the nature of the note and deed of trust.

The settlement attorney is normally expected to prepare any promissory note involved in the closing. Form notes are available from a variety of sources such as the VA, FHA and lenders. The note is not recorded. The purchaser/borrower is the maker; the lender is the holder. Only one note is needed per loan in the usual situation. The note and deed of trust should be signed in the exact manner and in the same name as the title is held. No witnesses are necessary. The deed of trust must, however, be acknowledged to permit its recordation in the land records of the circuit court where the property is located. Further, VA and FHA notes and notes to be sold out-of-state require notarization; therefore, many note forms provide space for notarization.

In most cases, the first payment of principal and interest will be due on the first day of the second month following month of closing. Most fixed-term residential loans are set up this way. The final payment is due on the first day of the last month of the loan term. For example, on a 30-year loan the final payment is due on the first day of the 360th month following the month of the closing. Thus for a loan closed January 20, 1988, the first payment will be due March 1, 1988, and the final payment will be due February 1, 2018. Other loans will involve various types of payment provisions.

### Prepayment Penalties

Virginia law provides that the following prepayment penalties are permissible for real estate loans:

1.   Home loans without regard to amount and when the home is occupied by the borrower:  two percent of the prepayment amount

2.   Other home loans under $75,000:  one percent of the unpaid principal

3.   Other home loans of $75,000 or more:  as agreed by the parties

It is not clear whether Virginia law permits partial prepayments and, if so, how one computes the prepayment penalty on multiple partial prepayments.

### Points

A *point* as used by real estate salesperson and brokers is defined as one percent of the loan amount. Since points are a part of the cost of obtaining a loan, the number of points charged on a conventional loan will vary according to the money market at the time the loan is committed. The real estate professional should monitor "where points are" for any particularday. For example, one day the interest rate on a particular loan may be ten percent, with three points; the next day, if the money market changes, the rate/point combination may be ten percent with five points. Obviously, it is to all parties' advantage to "lock in" (i.e., obtain the lender's commitment) when the points are low. The real estate professional should be prepared to consult and advise the purchaser as to when to lock in. A contract typically provides that the purchaser will pay the points to the lender or that the seller will pay any points charged in excess of a stated percentage of the loan amount. The seller's agent should put a ceiling on the number of points a seller is obligated to pay.

As a practical matter, there also is no limit on the points that can be charged to the buyer. Points may be considered as additional interest, and no ceiling exists on the amount of interest to be charged on a first deed of trust if stated in the loan contract or truth-in-lending disclosure statement. The purchaser must pay the points directly to the lender at closing, or the settlement agent or attorney must collect the entire loan proceeds from the lender and pay the points back to the lender. Otherwise, the IRS will not treat the points paid as interest for purposes of calculating the purchaser's interest deduction for personal income tax.

## Late Charges

Most conventional first deed of trust loans will contain a provision for a late charge in the event a monthly payment is not made within a certain period of time after the due date. The fact that a late charge may be collected must be disclosed in the truth-in-lending disclosure. Virginia law provides that a late charge may not exceed five percent of the installment due and cannot be collected unless the payment is not made within seven calendar days after the due date. To be collected, the late charge must be specified in the contract between the lender (or seller) and the purchaser/debtor. Late charges in excess of the amount permitted by Virginia law are void as to the excess but do not otherwise affect the obligation.

## Escrows

In a clause in the deed of trust (and sometimes also the note) lenders may require the borrower to pay into "escrow" at settlement the real estate taxes for a number of months, which together with taxes included with each monthly payment under the note will give the lender sufficient funds to pay the local real estate tax bills before they become due. This ensures that the taxes do not become delinquent and a prior lien on the property. Otherwise, the property could be sold for delinquent taxes and the lien of the deed of trust would be extinguished by a sale pursuant to a superior lien.

The lender will usually require the borrower to purchase a hazard insurance policy, include the name of the lender in the "loss payee" clause or as an additional insured and furnish a paid receipt for the first year's premium. Many lenders require the escrow of two-twelfths of the annual premium and collect one month's premium with each monthly payment of the note so that they may pay the premium before its due date. Some lenders, however, allow the borrower to renew the insurance annually and furnish the lender evidence of such renewal before each expiration date. Obviously, hazard insurance is extremely important to mortgage lenders because it insures preservation of the value of the security for the loan.

## Other Charges

Virginia law permits service charges or "origination fees" on all real estate loans in the amount of $20 or one percent, whichever is greater. Virginia law also authorizes the lender to require the borrower to pay other reasonable and necessary charges in connection with making the loan, including the cost of title examination, title insurance, recording charges, taxes, hazard insurance, mortgage guarantee insurance, appraisals, credit reports, surveys, document preparation, real estate tax service fees, lender inspection fees and closing the loan.

The lender generally will require a house location survey dated not more than six months prior to settlement and prepared by a certified land surveyor. Many borrowers object to the charge when an existing survey can be produced and furnished to the lender. It can be argued that for a sale of an existing residence, the lender should be satisfied with an existing survey, coupled with an affidavit by the seller, stating that since the date of the survey no additions had been made to the house, nor had any buildings, fences or other improvements been constructed there or onto neighboring lots. However, lenders generally insist on receiving an updated survey.

## FHA FINANCING

Since FHA-insured loans are treated fully in the main text, a few details will suffice here.

## Assumption

FHA loans are fully assumable within their first 24 months with FHA approval of the credit of the purchaser assuming the loan and are fully assumable at any time thereafter. There is no clause in the FHA deed of trust that prohibits assumption or allows the noteholder to accelerate the note in the event of sale.

Note that the paragraph at the top of the second column of page 2 of the FHA deed of trust dealing with the disbursement of foreclosure proceeds is inconsistent with Virginia law (which controls), which requires the trustee to satisfy inferior liens of record prior to disbursing any surplus proceeds to the owner. Note also that paragraph 2 on page 3 of the form provides for the establishment of an escrow fund for the payment by the noteholder of the mortgage insurance premium when the note is so insured; however, FHA now requires that the total mortgage insurance premium be paid in advance (or the full premium may be financed with the loan).

## Late Charges

FHA regulations provide for the collection by the lender of a late charge not to exceed four cents for each dollar of each payment that is more than 15 days late. Late charges must be charged separately to and collected from the mortgagor and cannot be deducted from any aggregate monthly payment.

Figure 15.1: Sample of Deed of Trust

| Commonwealth of Virginia | **Deed of Trust** | FHA Case No.: |
| --- | --- | --- |

**This Deed of Trust**, made this                     day of                     , in the year 19   , between

party of the first part, and
and                                                                                                Trustee, of

party of the second part:

Witnesseth, that the said party of the first part does grant with General Warranty unto the said party of the second part the following property, in the                     of                     , County of
and State of Virginia to wit:

**And It is Mutually Understood and Agreed** by and between the parties hereto that all the buildings, walks, fences, shrubbery, driveways, improvements and fixtures of every kind, including stoves, refrigerators, ranges, cabinets, venetian blinds, heaters, boilers, radiators, engines, machines, motors, screens, blinds, doors, hardware, wires, switches, electric fixtures, bells, insulations, and all other water, plumbing, ventilating, and heating equipment, including stokes, oil burners, tanks, air conditioning equipment now upon or which may hereafter be placed upon said property, shall be deemed to be fixtures and part of the realty herein conveyed, and shall be deemed part of the security for the indebtedness herein mentioned, and shall be covered by this deed of trust.

**In Trust** to secure to

a corporation organized and existing under the laws of
or its assigns, the payment of certain promissory note bearing even date herewith in the principal sum of
                                        Dollars ($                     ),
with interest from date at the rate of                     per centum (          %)
per annum on the unpaid balance until paid, and made by
                                payable to the order of

at its office in
or at such other place as the holder may designate in writing, the said principal and interest being payable in monthly installments of
                                        Dollars ($                     ),
on the first day of                     , 19   , and a like sum on the first day of each and every month thereafter until the note
is fully paid, except that the entire indebtedness evidenced by said note, if not sooner paid, shall be due and payable on the first day of
                     , 20   .

Courtesy of Southgate Mortgage Corporation, Virginia Beach, VA.

### Figure 15.1: Sample of Deed of Trust (Continued)

Also upon the further trust that the said party of the first part shall remain in quiet and peaceable possession of the above-granted and described premises, and take the profits thereof to his own use, until default be made in the payment of any matter of indebtedness hereby secured or in the performance of any of the covenants herein provided; and, also, to secure the reimbursement to the holder of said note and to the party hereto of the second part, or substitute Trustees, or Trustee, and any purchaser or purchasers under any sale or sales as provided by this Trust, for any and all costs and expenses incurred in respect thereto, including reasonable counsel fees incurred or paid on account of any litigation at law or in equity which may arise in respect to this Trust, or to the indebtedness on the property heretofore mentioned, and counsel fees incurred or paid by any reason of any condemnation or eminent domain proceeding in which the property hereby conveyed is involved or described, or in obtaining possession of the premises after any sale which may be made as hereinafter provided for.

In the event that default shall be made in the payment of the note secured hereby or of any monthly installment of principal and interest as therein provided for, or in the payment of any of the monthly sums for taxes, special assessments, mortgage, fire and other hazard insurance, all as hereinafter provided; or upon any default on payment on demand of any money advanced by the holder of said note on account of any proper cost, charge, commission, or expense in and about the same, or on account of any tax or assessment or insurance, or expense of litigation, with interest thereon at the rate set forth in the note secured hereby from date of such advance (it being hereby agreed that on default in the payment of any tax or assessment to insurance premium or any payment on account thereof, or in the payment of any said costs, expense of litigation, as aforesaid, the holder of said note may pay the same, and all sums so advanced, with interest as aforesaid, shall immediately attach as a lien hereunder, and be payable on demand), or upon failure or inability faithfully and fully to keep and perform any of the other conditions or covenants herein provided; then upon any and every such default so made as aforesaid it is expressly covenanted and agreed by said party of the first part that the holder of the note may, after thirty days default, treat the whole principal debt hereby secured as thereupon immediately due and payable, and shall in order to recover said principal debt or sum and interest thereon until paid, have the right then or thereafter at any time to sue thereon at law or in equity, or to enforce payment thereof by means of any remedies or provisions in these presents contained; and these rights shall exist notwithstanding that by the terms of said principal note it may not on its face be due.

In the event of default occurring as described in the preceding paragraph, then the Trustees, or any one of them, their successors or assigns, on being requested so to do by the holder of the note, shall sell for cash the property hereby conveyed after first advertising the time, terms, and place of sale for five times in some newspaper published in, or having a general circulation in, the county or city wherein the property lies, or by any other method of advertisement that the

Trustees may deem wise, which cash shall be distributed by the Trustees in the following manner, to wit:

So much of the proceeds as may be necessary to defray the expense of executing this Trust, including a Trustees' commission of

                        percentum (       %)

on the gross proceeds of sale hereunder, and all proper costs, charges, and expenses, including all attorney's and other fees, and costs herein provided for, and all moneys advanced for costs or expenses, or expense of litigation as aforesaid, of taxes or assessments or insurance, with interest thereon as aforesaid, and all taxes, general and special, and assessments, due upon said land and premises at the time of sale, and to discharge the amount of money then payable upon the said note according to its tenor; together with all interest accrued and to accrue thereon up to the date of payment of the purchase money by the purchaser at such sale. And the Trustees or Trustee, shall pay the remainder of said proceeds, if any, to the party of the first part, upon delivery of and surrender to the purchaser of possession of the premises as aforesaid, sold and conveyed, less the expense, if any, of obtaining possession. At any sale hereunder the Trustees, or the one acting shall have authority and at their or his discretion to require any bidder to deposit prior to receiving his bid or to knocking down the property to him a

bidder's deposit of not more than $         before his bid is received, which shall be refunded to the bidder unless the property is sold to him, otherwise to be applied to his credit in settlement, or should he fail to complete his purchase promptly, to be applied to pay the costs and expenses of sale and the balance, if any, to be retained by the Trustees, or the one acting on the Trustees' behalf, as their or his compensation in connection with the sale.

If at the time of sale the said Trustees, or the one acting, shall deem it best for any reason to postpone or continue said sale for one or more days, they or he may do so, in which event notice of such postponement or continuance shall be made in such manner as the Trustees, or the one acting, may deem sufficient. It is further agreed that if the said property shall be advertised for sale as herein provided and not sold, the Trustees, or the one acting, shall be entitled to a reasonable commission not exceeding one-half the commission above provided, to be computed on the amount of principal then unpaid.

In the event of the resignation, death, incapacity, disability, removal, or absence from the State of any Trustee or Trustees, or should either refuse to act or fail to execute this Trust when requested, then any other Trustee shall have all the rights, powers, and authority and be charged with the duties that are hereby conferred or charged upon both; and in such event, or at the option of the hold of the note and with or without cause, the holder of the note is hereby authorized and empowered to appoint, and to substitute and appoint, by an instrument recorded wherever this Deed of Trust is recorded, a Trustee in the place and stead of any Trustee herein named or any succeeding or substitute Trustee, which appointed and Substitute Trustee or Trustees shall have all the rights, powers, and authority and be charged with all the duties that are conferred or charged

Courtesy of Southgate Mortgage Corporation, Virginia Beach, VA.

Figure 15.1: Sample of Deed of Trust (Continued)

upon any Trustee or Trustees herein named.

. In addition to the causes hereinabove set forth for substitution of Trustee, the owner of the debt hereby secured, for any other reason satisfactory to such owner, is hereby empowered to appoint another trustee in the place and stead of said trustee or any successor in trust, and the title hereby conveyed to said trustee shall be vested in said new trustee. Such appointment shall be in writing and shall be duly recorded as aforesaid.

And the said party of the first part, in order more fully to protect the security of this Deed of Trust, does hereby covenant and agree as follows:

1. That he will promptly pay the principal of and interest on the indebtedness evidenced by said note, at the times and in the manner therein provided. Privilege is reserved to pay the debt in whole or in part on any installment due date.

2. That, together with and in addition to the monthly payment of principal and interest payable under the terms of the note secured hereby, he will pay to the holder of the note, on the first day of each month until it is fully paid, the following sums:

(a) A sum equal to the ground rents, if any, next due, plus the premiums that will next become due and payable on policies of fire and other hazard insurance covering the mortgaged property, plus taxes and assessments next due on the mortgaged property (all as estimated by the holder of the note) less all sums already paid therefor divided by the number of months to elapse before one (1) month prior to the date when such ground rents, premiums, taxes, and assessments will become delinquent, such sums to be held by the holder of the note in trust to pay said ground rents, premiums, taxes, and special assessments; and

(b) All payments mentioned in the preceding subsection of this paragraph and all payments to be made under the note secured hereby shall be added together and the aggregate amount thereof shall be paid by the party of the first part each month in a single payment to be applied by the holder of the note to the following items in the order set forth:

(I)   ground rents, taxes, special assessments, fire, and other hazard insurance premiums;
(II)  interest on the note secured hereby;
(III) amortization of the principal of said note; and
(IV)  late charges.

Any deficiency in the amount of such aggregate monthly payment shall, unless made good by the party of the first part prior to the due date of the next such payment, constitute an event of default under this Deed of Trust. The holder of the note may collect a "late charge" not to exceed four cents (4¢) for each dollar ($1) of each payment more than fifteen (15) days in arrears to cover the extra expense involved in handling delinquent payments.

3. If the total of the payments made by the party of the first part under (a) of paragraph 2 preceding shall exceed the amount of the payments actually made by the holder of the note secured hereby for ground rents, taxes, or assessments or insurance premiums, as the case may be, such excess, if the loan is current, at the option of the party of the first part, shall be credited on subsequent payments to be made by the party of the first part, or refunded to the party of the first part. If, however, the monthly payments made by the party of the first part, under (a) of paragraph 2 preceding, shall not be sufficient to pay ground rents, taxes and assessments, and insurance premiums, as the case may be, when the same shall become due and payable, then the party of the first part shall pay to the holder of said note any amount necessary to make up the deficiency, on or before the date when payment of such ground rents, taxes, assessments, or insurance premiums shall be due. If at any time the party of the first part shall tender to the holder of said note, in accordance with the provisions thereof, full payment of the entire indebtedness represented thereby, the said holder shall, in computing the amount of such indebtedness, credit to the account of the party of the first part any balance remaining in the funds accumulated under the provisions of (a) of paragraph 2 hereof. If there shall be a default under any of the provisions of this Deed of Trust resulting in a public sale of the premises covered hereby, or if the property is otherwise acquired after default, the holder of the note shall apply, at the time of the commencement of such proceedings, or at the time the property is otherwise acquired, the balance then remaining in the funds accumulated under: (a) of paragraph 2 preceding, as a credit against the amount of principal then remaining unpaid under said note.

4. That he will keep the improvements now existing or hereafter erected on the said premises, insured as may be required from time to time by the holder of the note against loss by fire in the sum of at least dollars and other hazards, casualties, and contingencies, in such amounts and for such periods as may be required by the holder of the note, and will pay promptly, when due any premiums on such insurance provision for the payment of which has not been made hereinbefore. All insurance shall be carried in companies approved by the holder of the note and the policies and renewals thereof shall be held by the holder of the note and have attached thereto mortgagee's clause without contribution in favor of and in form acceptable to the holder of the note. All such policies and renewals and all other policies issued and hereafter to be issued covering said premises are hereby assigned to the holder of the note as additional security for the payment of all sums and interest secured hereby. The party of the first part further covenants that in the event of his failure to keep the property so insured and the policies so deposited, then the holder of the note may at his option, but without any obligation to effect the same, effect such insurance and pay the premiums thereon and the money so paid, with interest thereon, shall become a part of the debt hereby secured, and shall be

Courtesy of Southgate Mortgage Corporation, Virginia Beach, VA.

Figure 15.1:  Sample of Deed of Trust  (Continued)

otherwise recoverable from the party of the first part as a debt. In the event of foreclosure of this Deed of Trust or other transfer of title to the said premises in extinguishment of the indebtedness secured hereby, all right, title, and interest of the party of the first part in and to any insurance policies then in force shall pass to the purchaser or grantee.

5.  That he will pay all taxes, assessments, water rates, and other governmental or municipal charges, fines, impositions, for which provision has not been made heretofore, and in default thereof the holder of the note secured hereby may pay the same; and that he will promptly deliver the official receipts therefore to the said holder.

6.  The party of the first part further assigns unto the holder of the note, as additional security, any rents which may now or hereafter be due upon the real estate above described, it being understood that in event it becomes necessary by reason of default under any of the terms hereof for the holder of the note to collect said rents, the holder of the note shall have the right and privilege of employing agents for that purpose and paying a percentage of the rents collected to such agents for such collection.

7.  That if the premises covered hereby, or any part thereof, shall be damaged by fire or other hazard against which insurance is held as hereinbefore provided, the amounts paid by any insurance company pursuant to the contract of insurance shall, to the extent of the indebtedness then remaining unpaid, be paid to the holder of the note secured hereby, and, at its option, may be applied to the debt or released for the repairing or rebuilding of the premises.

8.  That he will keep the said premises in as good order and condition as they are now and will not commit or permit any waste of the said premises, reasonable wear and tear excepted.

9.  That if the premises, or any part thereof, be condemned under any power of eminent domain, or acquired for a public use, the damages, proceeds, and the consideration for such acquisition, to the extent of the full amount of indebtedness upon this Deed of Trust, and the note secured hereby remaining unpaid, are hereby assigned by the party of the first part to the holder of the note and shall be paid

forthwith to the holder of the note to be applied by it on account of the indebtedness secured hereby, whether due or not.

10.  That should this Deed of Trust and the note secured hereby not be eligible for insurance under the National Housing Act within                    days from the date hereof (written statement of any officer of the Department of Housing and Urban Development or authorized agent of the Secretary of Housing and Urban Development dated subsequent to the                    days' time from the date of this Deed of Trust, declining to insure said note and this Deed of Trust, being deemed conclusive proof of such ineligibility), the holder of the note secured hereby may, at its option, declare all sums secured hereby immediately due and payable. Notwithstanding the foregoing, this option may not be exercised by the holder of the note secured hereby when the ineligibility for insurance under the National Housing Act is due to the holder of said note's failure to remit the mortgage insurance premium to the Department of Housing and Urban Development.

Notice of the exercise of any option granted herein, or in the note secured hereby, to the holder thereof, is not required to be given.

11.  Upon the full payment of said note, and the interest thereon, and all moneys advanced or expended, as herein provided, and all other proper costs, charges, commissions, half-commissions, and expenses, the party of the second part shall release and reconvey the above-described premises unto and at the cost of the party of the first part.

The party of the first part hereby waives the benefit of all homestead exemption as to the debt secured by this deed and as to any expenditure for insurance, taxes, levies, assessments, dues or charges, by the holder of the note in pursuance of this Deed of Trust.

The covenants herein contained shall bind, and the benefits and advantages shall inure to, the respective heirs, executors, administrators, successors, and assigns of the parties hereto. Whenever used, the singular number shall include the plural, the plural the singular, and the use of any gender shall include all other genders.

Witness the following signature(s) and seal(s).

_____ [SEAL]

_____ [SEAL]

_____ [SEAL]

_____ [SEAL]

013504                    Page 4 of 5                    HUD-92187M-1 (5-86 Edition)

Courtesy of Southgate Mortgage Corporation, Virginia Beach, VA.

Figure 15.1:  Sample of Deed of Trust  (Continued)

State of Virginia,                                   )
                                                     ) To Wit:
County of                                            )

   I,                                          , a Notary public for the
aforesaid in the State of Virginia, do certify that

                                              , whose name          signed to writing
above, bearing date on the          day of                  , 19    , ha    acknowledged
the same before me in my                                        and State aforesaid.

   Given under my hand this                     day of                  , 19       .

   My commission expires on the                 day of                  , 19       .

                                          _____
                                          Notary Public,                County, Virginia

   Received for Record on the          day of          , A.D.: 19    , at          o'clock    M.,
and recorded in Liber No.at folio          , one of the Land Records of the Commonwealth of Virginia, and examined by

                                          _____
                                                         Recorder

013504                          Page 5 of 5                    HUD-92187M-1 (5-86 Edition)

Courtesy of Southgate Mortgage Corporation, Virginia Beach, VA.

Figure 15.2: Sample Deed of Trust Note

| State of Virginia | **Deed of Trust Note** | FHA Case Number: |
|---|---|---|

$                                                                   , Virginia,
                                                                     , 19    .

**For Value Received,** the undersigned promise(s) to pay to

or order, the principal sum of

                                                        Dollars ($          ),
with interest from date at the rate of                    . per centum (      %)
per annum on the unpaid balance until paid. The said principal and interest shall be payable at the office of

                                                                        , in

or at such other place as the holder hereof may designate in writing, in monthly installments of

                                                        Dollars ($          ),
commencing on the first day of                  , 19    , and on the first day of each month thereafter until the principal and interest are fully paid, except that the entire indebtedness evidenced hereby, if not sooner paid, shall be due and payable on the first day of                  , 20

If default be made in the payment of any installment under this Note, and if such default is not made good prior to the due date of the next such installment, the entire principal sum and accrued interest shall at once become due and payable without notice at the option of the holder of this Note. Failure to exercise this option shall not constitute a waiver of the right to exercise the same in the event of any subsequent default.

Presentment, protest, and notice are hereby waived. The drawers and endorsers of this Note also waive the benefit of the homestead exemption as to this debt.

This Note and the interest are secured by the first Deed of Trust of even date herewith on property located in                  County, Virginia, and this Note is to be construed according to the laws of Virginia.

_____       _____

_____       _____

**This is to Certify** that this is the Note described in and secured by Deed of Trust of even date herewith, and in the same principal amount as herein stated, to
                                                        , trustee(s), on real estate
located in                  County, Virginia.

Dated                            , 19

_____
*(Notary Public)*

This form is used in connection with deeds of trust insured under the one- to four-family provisions of the National Housing Act.

Form HUD-99187 dated (10-78) may be used until supply is exhausted.              HUD-99187(10-78 Edition) Reprinted 6-85

Courtesy of Southgate Mortgage Corporation, Virginia Beach, VA.

Figure 15.3: Sample of FHA Deed of Trust Rider

```
                    FHA ASSUMPTION POLICY RIDER


     THIS RIDER is made this _____day of _____,
     19___, and is incorporated into and shall be deemed to amend and
     supplement the Mortgage, Deed of Trust or Security Deed ( the
     "Security Instrument") of even date herewith, given by the undersigned
     (the "Borrower") to secure Borrower's Note to SOUTHGATE MORTGAGE
     CORPORATION (the "Lender") of the same date and covering the property
     described in the Security Instrument and located at
     _____.


          In addition to the covenants and agreements made in the Security
     Instrument, Borrower and Lender further covenant and agree as follows:

               The mortgagee shall, with the prior approval of
               the Federal Housing Commissioner, or his designee
               declare all sums secured by this mortgage to be
               immediately due and payable if all or part of the
               property is sold or otherwise transferred (other
               than by devise, descent or operation of law) by
               the mortgagor, pursuant to a contract of sale
               executed not later than _____months after the
               date on which the mortgage is executed, to a
               purchaser whose credit has not been approved in
               accordance with the requirements of the Commissioner.


          BY SIGNING BELOW, BORROWER accepts and agrees to the terms and
     provisions contained in this Rider.



                         _____
                         Borrower

                         _____
                         Borrower



     SMC 3/13/89
```

Courtesy of Southgate Mortgage Corporation, Virginia Beach, VA.

Figure 15.4: Sample of VA Deed of Trust Rider

VA DEED OF TRUST RIDER

THIS LOAN IS NOT ASSUMABLE WITHOUT THE APPROVAL OF THE VETERANS ADMINISTRATION
OR ITS AUTHORIZED AGENT

This rider is made this _____ day of _____, 19___, and is incorporated into and shall be deemed to amend and supplement the Deed of Trust/Mortgage (the "Security Instrument") of the same date given by the undersigned, Party of the First Part to secure said Party's Note to Southgate Mortgage Corporation, Holder of the Note of the same date and covering the property described in the Security Instrument and located at:

_____
(property address)

AMENDMENTS TO COVENANTS. Party of the First Part and Holder of the Note agree that the following covenants are added and made a part of the covenants made in the Security Instrument.

THIS LOAN IS IMMEDIATELY DUE AND PAYABLE UPON TRANSFER OF THE PROPERTY SECURING SUCH LOAN TO ANY TRANSFEREE, UNLESS THE ACCEPTABILITY OF THE ASSUMPTION OF THE LOAN IS ESTABLISHED PURSUANT TO SECTION 1817A OF CHAPTER 37, TITLE 38, UNITED STATES CODE.

FUNDING FEE. A fee equal to one-half of one percent of the balance of this loan as of the date of transfer of the property shall be payable at the time of transfer to the loan holder or its authorized agent, as trustee for the Administrator of Veterans Affairs.  If the assumer fails to pay this fee at the time of transfer, the fee shall constitute an additional debt to that already secured by this instrument, shall bear interest at the rate herein provided, and, at the option of the payee of the indebtedness hereby secured or any transferee thereof, shall be immediately due and payable. This fee is automatically waived if the assumer is exempt under the provisions of 38 U.S.C. 1829 (b).

PROCESSING CHARGE. Upon application for approval to allow assumption of this loan, a processing fee may be charged by the loan holder or its authorized agent for determining the creditworthiness of the assumer and subsequently revising the holder's ownership records when an approved transfer is completed.  The amount of this charge shall not exceed the maximum established by the Veterans Administration for a loan to which Section 1817A, Chapter 37, Title 38, United States Code applies.

INDEMNITY LIABILITY. If this obligation is assumed, then the assumer hereby agrees to assume all of the obligations of the veteran under the terms of the instruments creating and securing the loan, including the obligation of the veteran to indemnify the Veterans Administration to the extent of any claim payment arising from the guaranty or insurance of the indebtedness created by this instrument.

IN WITNESS WHEREOF, the said Mortgagor has hereunto set his hand and seal this day and year first aforesaid.

Signed, sealed and delivered    _____

_____

STATE OF _____
CITY/COUNTY OF _____, to-wit:

I, _____, a Notary Public for the

City/County and State aforesaid, do certify that _____

_____ whose name(s) is/are signed to the above, has/have

acknowledged the same before me this _____ day of _____, 19_____.

_____        MY COMMISSION EXPIRES: _____
        (Notary Public)

## VA FINANCING

VA-guaranteed loans are treated fully in the main text; however, brief remarks are given below.

### Late Charges

If the loan document so provides, a lender may collect a late charge not in excess of four percent of a monthly payment made more than 15 days overdue.  However, a late charge may not be deducted from a regular installment.

### Other Charges

The VA lender's handbook provides that no other charges may be made against or paid by the borrower except those expressly permitted by the VA.  Reasonable and customary charges are permitted for the following:  (1) examination of title and title insurance; (2) recording fees, taxes and other charges incident to recordation; (3) hazard insurance for at least one year; (4) VA appraisal fee; (5) credit report; (6) survey, except such charges for condominiums must have prior approval by the VA; (7) interest from date of settlement to the first of next month; and (8) construction loan advance fee.

No charge may be made to the borrower for the following:  (1) preparation of deed of trust and note; (2) settlement fee; (3) notary fee; (4) brokerage or service fees; (5) life insurance premiums; and (6) cost normally attributable to seller.  The seller may be charged for preparation of the deed, settlement or attorney's fees, release of existing trusts, points and lender's inspection fee.  In the past, the VA has also permitted the seller to be charged for the preparation of the note and deed of trust and the settlement fee.

## CREDIT LINE DEEDS OF TRUST

Virginia law provides for a credit line deed of trust provided the document contains on the front page in capital underscored type:  THIS IS A CREDIT LINE DEED OF TRUST.  This phrase will convey notice that the noteholder named in the deed of trust and the grantors and other borrowers identified in the deed of trust have an agreement:  the noteholder may make advances from time to time secured by the real estate described in the deed of trust in a total amount not to exceed the maximum credit line extended to the borrower.  From the date of the recording of a credit line deed of trust, the lien has priority over (1) all other deeds, conveyances and other instruments or contracts in writing, which are unrecorded at that time and of which the noteholder has no knowledge; and (2) judgment liens subsequently docketed.  However, if a judgment creditor gives notice to the noteholder at the address indicated on the credit line deed of trust, the deed of trust has no priority over the judgment for any advances or extensions of credit subsequently made under the deed of trust.

## CONVENTIONAL MORTGAGE INSURANCE

While VA loans are guaranteed by the Veterans Administration and FHA loans are insured by the Federal Housing Administration, conventional loans are usually insured by private insurance companies. Most conventional lenders will require private mortgage insurance (PMI) when the loan amount is in excess of 80 percent of the appraised value. Such insured loans are no different from any other conventional loans except for the insurance. The cost of the insurance is substantial. Sometimes the purchaser is given the option as to how the premium is to be paid. The premium may be as much as one percent of the loan amount for the first year and as much as one-half percent per year thereafter. Two months' premium will be paid at settlement, and one month's premium will be paid with each monthly payment. These amounts are held by the lender in escrow to pay future premiums. The purchaser will also be required to sign a statement authorizing the lender to pay future premiums as they become due and to collect them from the borrower. Theoretically, when the loan amount has been reduced to 80 percent of the appraised value, the mortgage insurance should no longer be necessary. It is the discretion of the lender to determine when the insurance is no longer to be required.

## ASSUMPTION

A deed of trust is assumable unless prohibited by the terms of the instrument. In today's real estate market, due to the history of variable interest rates, conventional loans are assumable only with written consent of the lender. Assumption is permitted (provided the assumer qualifies) in VA loans and under certain conditions in FHA loans. The conventional lender will require a satisfactory credit report on the purchaser and will usually adjust the interest rate to the prevailing market rate if the rate is higher than the original rate. Moreover, the lender will generally charge an assumption fee of not more than one percent of the outstanding principal. Due-on-sale clauses are enforceable in Virginia.

### Required Notice

Virginia law provides that where a loan containing a due-on-sale clause is made on real property comprised of not more than four residential dwelling units, the deed of trust must contain the following language, either in capital letters or underlined: Notice--the debt secured hereby is subject to call in full or the terms thereof being modified in the event of sale or conveyance of the property conveyed. If such provisions appear, the real estate professional should advise the client of their effect.

### Assuming versus Taking "Subject To"

A distinction between a purchaser "assuming" a deed of trust as opposed to taking "subject to" a deed of trust is that in the former case the purchaser becomes personally liable for the debt and the covenants in the note and deed of trust, while in the latter case the purchaser assumes no personal liability.

## Modification in Release

If any of the terms of the loan to be assumed are to be modified, the lender should require a separate *modification agreement* to be executed by the original grantors, makers, endorsers, trustees and the noteholder.  This is necessary to prevent discharge of the liability of any of the original obligors by operation of suretyship law.

## Advantages of Assumption

The assumption or taking subject to of an existing deed of trust is the quickest and most economical means of financing the purchase of a home.  The purchaser will have to pay the balance of the purchase price or pay part cash and secure the balance with a purchase-money second deed of trust with the seller or third party.  Such a settlement can be accomplished quickly, because it involves no new financing from a commercial lender.  The only delay involved might be in obtaining assumption figures from the holder of the deed of trust to be assumed.  It is an economical method of financing:  the interest rate of the loan to be assumed is frequently lower than the prevailing interest rate, and no charges need to be paid to lender (except perhaps an assumption fee).  There will be no recording charges for a new lien first deed of trust, and no cost of releasing an existing deed of trust.  The lender often does not require appraisals, credit reports, a new survey or similar items representing additional expenses.  In addition, *the grantor's tax on the deed of assumption is based only upon the equity,* which is the purchase price less the balance of the deed of trust assumed.

# PURCHASE-MONEY FINANCING

A deed of trust given with the conveyance of land to secure the unpaid balance of the purchase price is called a purchase-money deed of trust.  The deed of trust should be labeled "Purchase-Money Deed of Trust."  A purchase-money deed of trust has priority over all other claims or liens arising through the mortgagor even if they are prior in time.  Prior judgments against the purchaser will not come ahead of the purchase-money deed of trust.  If the purchaser is married and takes title to the property in his or her name alone, the purchaser's spouse will not have to execute a purchase-money deed of trust because dower and curtesy interests are inferior to the purchase-money deed of trust.

# DEFERRED PURCHASE-MONEY DEED OF TRUST

A useful device, particularly when the seller is an older person or installment sale tax treatment is desired, is a substantial down payment with a *deferred* purchase-money deed of trust held by the seller.  Such an arrangement may be prohibited, however, if there is to be a first deed of trust to an outside (institutional) lender.  A purchase-money deed of trust held by the seller should state that it is granted to secure *deferred* purchase money, whereas a purchase-money deed of trust to a third party will state that it is granted to secure purchase money.  If it is a second deed of trust, it will generally be for a short term with a balloon payment at the end.  If it is subordinated, the purchase-money deed of trust should include a provision that any default in a senior encumbrance or lien will also be considered a default on a purchase-money deed of trust.

## RELEASES

Where a large tract of land is being financed and developed and the sale of the tract in similar parcels is contemplated, the real estate professional should consider requesting the attorney to put a provision in the deed of trust allowing for partial releases.  For the lender's protection, it is wise to state that the parcels to be released shall be contiguous to each other; that the amount of the consideration based upon a figure *in excess* of a pro rata portion of the purchase price per acre shall be paid off for each release; that portions of the land that are more valuable due to topography or improvements are not subject to release; or any other provisions to protect the lender from a developer who might sell off the best portions, leaving the lender holding security worth less than the remaining debt.  The borrower should be entitled to obtain a release of roadways and other such improvements without payment of release fee, provided the borrower has posted the appropriate bonds with the county or city and otherwise demonstrated to the lender the ability to pay for such improvements.  Whenever the borrower pays off any note, a marginal release is made in the deed book and page on the face of the instrument where the document is recorded, or a certificate of satisfaction or partial satisfaction form is filed in the deed books in the clerk's office where the land is located.

## VIRGINIA HOUSING DEVELOPMENT AUTHORITY

The Virginia Housing Development Authority (VHDA) extends loans to residents of the Commonwealth of Virginia under the following conditions:

1.  The buyer cannot have owned a home during the three years prior to making the application for the loan.

2.  Private mortgage insurance is required until the loan is paid down to 80 percent of the value of the property.

3.  If the loan is a VHDA-VA loan, the VHDA will lend the entire purchase price and no down payment shall be required to be made by the borrower.  Other VHDA loan programs require small down payments.

4.  The seller must pay the single discount point.

5.  A power of attorney cannot be used in executing the documents; rather, both parties must personally execute all VHDA documents.

6.  In a 1988 legislative assembly, the VHDA law was changed to the effect that the VHDA can now build and operate residential building and nursing care facilities and nursing homes.  Further, the definition of "housing development" "housing project," and "residential housing" now provides that medical and related facilities for the residence and care of the aged are deemed to be dwelling accommodations for the purpose of the act.

## FORECLOSURE

There are three ways to foreclose a deed of trust in Virginia:

1. Decree of court (strict foreclosure);

2. Conveyance of the property by the grantors and the trustees to the beneficiary in consideration of the whole or part of the debt ("deed in lieu of foreclosure"); and

3. Sale by the trustee pursuant to a power of sale ("trustee sale").

While an exhaustive discussion of foreclosure procedures is not necessary here, it is nonetheless important for the licensee to be aware that bankruptcy of the mortgagor is an automatic stay of foreclosure. If a lien is foreclosed (i.e., no bankruptcy was granted), the lien and all inferior liens are wiped out; however, superior liens (those having priority over the foreclosed lien) are not affected, and a purchaser would take the property subject to such liens.

### Trustee's Powers and Duties

Legal title to the property conveyed by the deed of trust is vested in the trustee for the benefit of the noteholder. Virginia is a "title theory" state as opposed to a "mortgage" or "lien theory" state. The trustee can act only in a manner authorized by statute or the express or implied terms of the trust.

The trustee is the agent for both the grantor (the homeowner) and the beneficiary (the lender) and is bound to act impartially between them (see Conflict of Interest). The trustee should bring the property to sale under every possible advantage to the trust. This includes using all reasonable diligence to obtain the best price under the circumstances. The trustee may adjourn the sale from time to time to meet any unexpected occurrences, but the readvertisement of the sale must be in the same manner as the original advertisements.

If only sham bidders are present at the sale and if the property would be sold at a grossly inadequate price resulting in a sacrifice of the property, it is the trustee's duty to adjourn the sale. In addition, if there are facts known that might have the effect of depressing the bidding, such as a cloud on title, the trustee must adjourn the sale and remove the hindrance, by suit if necessary.

By statute in Virginia, the trustee must ascertain whether there are any real estate tax liens against the property being sold; Virginia law obligates the trustee to pay the taxes out of the proceeds of sale and gives the tax lien priority over the deed of trust. In addition, Virginia law requires the *purchaser* to see that the taxes are paid. If the taxes are not paid, the trustee may be liable personally and the purchaser takes the land subject to the tax lien (though not personally liable for its payment). The trustee should also pay to the appropriate body the prorated portion of the current year's real estate taxes.

### Other Encumbrances

The rule of "buyer beware" as to the quality of both title and the property applies in foreclosure sales.

## Advertisement

The terms of the deed of trust will determine how the property is advertised. Even if the number of advertisements meets these terms, state law provides that the sale may take place no earlier than the eighth day after the first advertisement and no later than 30 days after the last advertisement.

## Conflict of Interest

A trustee may not purchase the property held in trust without written permission from the mortgagor. The trustee is bound by law to secure the highest possible price for the property, whereas purchaser seeks to do the opposite. The trustee's duty to the trust transcends any potential personal interest he may have or acquire in the property.

## Auction

The sale must be held in accordance with the terms of the deed of trust, which specifies the time, manner and place of sale. Unless the deed of trust states otherwise, the property is sold at the "premises or in front of the circuit court building or at such other place in the city or county as the trustee may select." At the sale, the trustee should sell the property to the highest bidder, have the successful purchaser execute a memorandum of sale and obtain the deposit from the purchaser.

## Trustee's Deed

The trustee cannot sell a greater interest than the deed of trust gives authority to sell, and the sale is subject to encumbrances having priority over the deed of trust. Accordingly, the trustee's deed should contain only a special warranty of title. However, the form of the deed and the title conveyed must conform to the manner in which the property was advertised.

## Disbursement of Proceeds

Virginia law provides that the trustee must apply the proceeds of sale in the following order: (1) to discharge the expenses of executing the trust, including a commission to the trustee of five percent of the gross proceeds of sale; (2) to discharge all taxes, levies and assessments with costs and interest, if they have priority over the deed of trust; (3) to discharge, in the order of their priority, any remaining debts and obligations secured by the deed of trust and any liens of record inferior to the deed of trust, with interest; and (4) to render the residue of the proceeds to the grantor or his assigns. When the sale is made under any recorded deed of trust, the trustee must file a report and accounting to the commissioner of accounts within four months of the sale.

## FHA and VA Limitations on Foreclosure

A lender or trustee foreclosing on a FHA or VA loan should be aware that such agencies require that the loan be in default for three months prior to the lender commencing foreclosure. In addition, they require that certain notices be given to the debtor and the insuring agency and that affirmative steps on the part of the lender be taken to attempt to avoid foreclosure, including setting up personal interviews and accepting partial payments.

## USURY

A usurious transaction generally is defined as the contract for the loan of money at a greater rate of interest than allowed by law.

It has been held that the taking of a ten-year exclusive-sales-agency contract on land in addition to the six percent interest (maximum rate at the time) as consideration for the making of a loan was usurious. In addition, where a loan was made at a six percent interest rate with an option to the lender to purchase the land at a price greatly below the market value, the loan was held to be usurious.

### Allowable Interest Rates on First Deed of Trust Loans

Virginia law provides that loans secured by a first deed of trust on real estate may be lawfully enforced with no limitation on the amount of interest, if it is properly stated in the instrument or separate agreement. The contract generally is considered to be the promissory note. Most prudent lenders insert the rate in the note. Virginia law provides that disclosure of charges may be contained in an interest disclosure statement if it is not otherwise specified in the note. Virginia law also provides that an interest rate that varies in accordance with any exterior standard or that cannot be ascertained from the contract without reference to exterior circumstances or documents is enforceable as agreed in the signed contract. For example, a note providing for an interest rate of three percent above the stated prime rate of a bank would be enforceable.

### Allowable Interest Rates Imposed or Collected by Sellers

Where the seller in a bona fide real estate transaction takes back a purchase-money deed of trust, the promissory note may provide for any rate of interest agreed to by the parties. Usury is not applicable to such a transaction because the interest rate is considered a time-price differential and thus part of the purchase price.

### Contracts or Notes in Violation of Virginia Usury Law Are Void

Any contract, note or deed of trust made or received, in providing for interest charges in excess of those permitted by Virginia law, shall be null and void and unenforceable by the lender or its assignees.

## WET SETTLEMENT ACT

The Wet Settlement Act applies to transactions involving purchase-money loans secured by first deeds of trust on real estate containing not more than four residential dwelling units.  The Act applies only to lenders regularly engaged in making loans secured by real estate.

At or before the loan closing, the lender shall disburse the loan proceeds to the settlement agent.  The lender may not charge or receive interest on the loan until disbursement of the loan funds and the loan closing have occurred.

The settlement agent or attorney will have the deed, deed of trust and any other necessary document recorded and will disburse the settlement proceeds within *two* business days of settlement.  A settlement agent or attorney may *not* disburse any loan funds prior to recording the deed of trust or other security instrument perfecting the lender's security instrument.  This change in the law occurred in 1987.  As a result, the real estate professional's commission check will not be given at the closing table but rather after the documents have been recorded by the settlement agent.

Any person who suffers the loss or failure by the lender or settlement agent to disburse as required by law will be entitled to recover, in addition to actual damages, double the amount of any interest collected plus reasonable attorney's fees.

## QUESTIONS

1.    Jake has bought a new house and is getting a new conventional loan.  Closing is June 15.  Normally his first mortgage payment would be due on what date?

   a.   June 15
   b.   July 1
   c.   July 15
   d.   August 1

2.    On a first deed of trust, what is the maximum interest that may be charged according to Virginia law?

   a.   No limit if the charge is stated in the loan contract
   b.   18% per annum
   c.   20% per annum
   d.   2% per month

3.    According to Virginia law, what is the maximum late charge that may be assessed?

   a.   No limit if the charge is stated in the loan contract
   b.   5%
   c.   10%
   d.   15%

4.    Which of the following is true of assumptions of deeds of trust in Virginia?

    a.    The grantor's tax is based on the equity only.
    b.    Assumptions can often be closed more quickly than new loans.
    c.    Appraisal, credit report and survey are not ordinarily required.
    d.    All of the above


5.    Which of the following is true of VHDA loans?

    a.    This program is primarily for those who already own a home.
    b.    The buyer must pay all discount points.
    c.    A power of attorney cannot be used to execute documents.
    d.    All of the above


6.    When a borrower in Virginia signs a note and deed of trust, what has he agreed to regarding a court hearing if he defaults?

    a.    To request the hearing within 30 days of default notice
    b.    To permit the lender to set the place and time of the hearing
    c.    To waive the hearing
    d.    To abide by the court's ruling without appeal


7.    In Virginia, a note and a deed of trust, respectively, must be:

    a.    acknowledged, recorded.
    b.    notarized, acknowledged.
    c.    acknowledged, notarized.
    d.    recorded, acknowledged.


8.    Which of the following statements is *not* true concerning prepayment penalties for real estate loans?

    a.    Virginia law sets up a definite schedule for partial prepayments.
    b.    For owner-occupied homes, the maximum penalty is 2% of the prepayment amount.
    c.    For home loans other than owner-occupied under $75,000, the maximum prepayment penalty is 1% of the unpaid principal.
    d.    For home loans other than owner-occupied over $75,000, the maximum prepayment penalty is as agreed by the parties.


9.    With regard to real estate loans, the term "locking in" refers to:

    a.    the buyer's closing date.
    b.    discount points charged by the lender.
    c.    the exact date of buyer's possession of the property.
    d.    lender's commitment to a precise loan amount.

10. What is the maximum number of discount points that may be charged to the buyer?

   a. 4
   b. 4 on first deeds of trust, no limit on seconds
   c. 8 on first deeds of trust, 4 on seconds
   d. No limit

11. How recent must the survey be that the lender requires before lending on a property?

   a. No survey required
   b. Within the past 30 days
   c. Within the past six months
   d. Within the previous owner's term of ownership, if he did not get a new first deed of trust when buying the property

12. For VA and FHA loans in Virginia, the maximum late charge is:

   a. 3% of the payment amount.
   b. 4% of the payment amount.
   c. 5% of the payment amount.
   d. as agreed by the parties (i.e., no legal limit).

13. Jill is granted a $40,000 maximum for a creditline deed of trust. She borrows $15,000 against it and then receives notice that a judgment for $10,000 has been docketed against her. She then withdraws $12,000 to pay other creditors; this amount is a new advance against her creditline deed of trust. The judgment creditor forecloses. Assuming the sale of the property brings enough money, what is the order in which the various amounts will be paid?

   a. $15,000, $10,000, $12,000
   b. $15,000, $12,000, $10,000
   c. $27,000, $10,000
   d. $10,000, $27,000

14. What happens to the borrower's PMI (private mortgage insurance) when the LTV falls to or below 80 percent?

   a. It is refunded.
   b. It continues as before.
   c. It is automatically terminated, with no refund.
   d. The lender may terminate the PMI at the lender's discretion.

15. FHA and VA loans in Virginia are assumable under which conditions?

   a. They are immediately and universally assumable.
   b. Both require the buyer to qualify at any time during the term of the loan.
   c. Both require the buyer to qualify during the first year or two of the loan.
   d. Neither may now be assumed under any circumstances.

16. Compared to the responsibilities of one who assumes a loan, the responsibilities of a buyer who takes a property subject to the loan are:

   a. identical.
   b. greater.
   c. less.
   d. greater during the first two years after the transfer, less thereafter.

17. The following are claims against a mortgagor; pick the one that has highest priority.

   a. Purchase-money deed of trust, 1980
   b. Judgment, docketed 1978
   c. Mechanic's lien, 1988
   d. Institutional mortgage, 1983

18. Walters sold land to a developer/builder who wishes to build homes on a few parcels at a time. Which of the following would place Walters' interest as mortgagee in the property at highest risk?

   a. Partial release of contiguous parcels
   b. Partial release of noncontiguous parcels
   c. Subordination of contiguous parcels
   d. Subordination of the entire tract

19. Which of the following is *not* a legal method of foreclosure in Virginia?

   a. Strict foreclosure
   b. Judicial foreclosure
   c. Nonjudicial foreclosure
   d. Deed in lieu of foreclosure

20. For purposes of the Virginia Housing Development Authority, facilities for residence and care of the aged are now classified as:

   a. commercial property.
   b. dwelling accommodations.
   c. nonconforming use that may survive conveyance.
   d. appropriate for conditional use permits.

21. Gramble's deed of trust is in default; foreclosure proceedings have begun. Gramble declares bankruptcy. What effect does this have on the foreclosure proceeding?

   a. No effect
   b. It brings about foreclosure immediately, since the advertisement rule is suspended in such a case.
   c. It reserves a homestead exemption for Gramble.
   d. It is an automatic stay of foreclosure (i.e., the proceedings come to an immediate halt).

22.    If the trustee at a foreclosure sale learns that only sham bidders are present and the sale price is likely to be quite low, what should he do?

a.    Adjourn the sale.
b.    Hold the sale as advertised.
c.    Purchase the property himself, with obligation to resell and escrow any profits for the benefit of the original mortgagor and mortgagee.
d.    Hold the sale and immediately docket the deficiency as a lien against the mortgagor.

23.    At a foreclosure, who is responsible to see to it that the general real estate tax has been paid?

a.    Mortgagor
b.    Mortgagee
c.    Trustee
d.    Purchaser

24.    At a foreclosure, who may be held personally liable if the general real estate taxes were not paid from the proceeds of the sale?

a.    Mortgagor
b.    Mortgagee
c.    Trustee
d.    Purchaser

25.    At a foreclosure sale, the trustee's deed is what type?

a.    General warranty
b.    Special warranty
c.    Bargain and sale
d.    Quitclaim

26.    For a VA or FHA loan, how long must the loan be in default before the trustee or lender can begin foreclosure proceedings?

a.    30 days
b.    Three months
c.    Six months
d.    No limit, it is at the lender's discretion.

27.    The Wet Settlement Act provides that:

a.    loans on wetlands require VHDA approval.
b.    "Time is of the essence" closings must have special provisions in case of weather-caused delays.
c.    all funds must be disbursed at settlement, prior to recording.
d.    all documents must be recorded prior to disbursement of funds.

ANSWERS

1.  d.  Interest is charged in arrears except for the month in which the buyer closes; he pays the remainder of June's interest in advance as a closing cost; July's interest is paid in the August 1 payment.

2.  a.

3.  b.

4.  d.

5.  c.

6.  c.  Virginia has nonjudicial foreclosures (no court hearing).

7.  b.  The note must be notarized if the loan is sold out-of-state; the deed of trust must be acknowledged to be eligible for recording.

8.  a.  It is unclear whether Virginia law permits partial prepayment.

9.  b.

10. d.

11. c.

12. b.

13. a.  Once the borrower has notice of the judgment, any further advances on the creditline deed of trust are inferior in priority to the judgment.

14. d.

15. c.

16.   c.   One who assumes a loan is responsible for the debt; one who takes it "subject to" agrees to make payments but is not responsible for the debt (i.e., it is nonrecourse financing).

17.   a.

18.   d.   If the developer obtains a construction loan as a first deed of trust and defaults, the property will probably not bring enough to pay the first, let alone the seller-held second.

19.   b.

20.   b.

21.   d.

22.   a.

23.   d.

24.   c.

25.   b.

26.   b.

27.   d.

# 16

## Leases

References to leases and the parties to them are scant and brief in the REB regulations; however, the Virginia Code (Vol. 8, pp. 235-80) treats leases and the landlord/tenant relationship in considerable depth. The portions relevant to prospective real estate licensees are summarized below.

### LEASING REAL ESTATE IN VIRGINIA

When property is conveyed subject to a valid lease, the new grantee stands in the same legal relation to the lessee as did the grantor of the property.

If a nonresident of Virginia owns real property consisting of four or more rental units (residential or commercial), he must appoint as agent a Virginia resident for the purpose of receiving any notices, service of process or other paper that would otherwise have been served on the owner. If such an agent is not appointed or if the one appointed cannot be found, the Secretary of the Commonwealth serves as agent and forwards any papers to be served on the owner to the owner's home address.

Virginia law requires three months' notice to terminate a year-to-year lease and 30 days for a month-to-month lease. Written notice of 120 days is required if the termination is due to rehabilitation of the property or to a change in use (such as conversion to a condominium, etc.); shorter notice may be arrived at by mutual written agreement.

If a tenant through no fault of his own is unable to vacate the premises at the end of the lease term, he is not legally held to another full term of the lease. He is liable to the lessor for use and occupation of the premises as well as any loss or damage caused to the lessor.

If a tenant whose rent is in arrears deserts the premises, the landlord may post a written notice in a conspicuous location on the premises requiring the tenant to pay the rent (in ten days for a monthly tenant and one month for a yearly tenant after the posting of the notice). If this is not done, the landlord may enter the premises, and the tenant's rights are at an end (though he still owes the rent up to the time of the landlord's reentry). For *residential* tenants, Virginia law specifies that failure to pay defaulted rents within five days of receiving notice ("five-day notice of pay or quit") results in the tenant's forfeiture of the right to possession.

In many states common law still governs statutes that require a lessee to be bound to lease terms and continue to pay full rent even if the improvements are destroyed on land that he rents. *Virginia has reversed and repealed this common-law doctrine.* If the tenant was not at fault in the destruction of the improvements, he is entitled to (at least) a reduction in the amount of rent until the improvements are rebuilt, so that the tenant's previous use of the property is restored.  While the tenant may be required to leave the property in good repair at the end of the lease, this not a covenant or obligation upon the tenant to rebuild in the event of destruction that was not his fault.  The landlord, however, also has no positive duty to rebuild; but the tenant is entitled to have the rent reduced proportional to the diminished value of the leased premises to the tenant for his purposes.  The tenant must prove that the destruction was not his fault and that the leased premises have been diminished in value to him.

Goods belonging to the tenant may be seized (distrained, distressed) for nonpayment of rent for up to five years after the rent is due, whether the lease has ended or not.  The seizure is made by a sheriff or other officer, based on a warrant from a judge or magistrate, the warrant in turn being based on a petition from the lessor stating the grounds for belief that the rent is due as well as the exact amount.  A copy of the distress warrant (order of seizure) is given to each defendant; the lessor must post bond and a copy of the bond must also be given to the delinquent lessee.  The goods subject to seizure include anything on the premises belonging to the tenant (or assignees or undertenants) or goods that have been removed within the 30 days prior to seizure.  If any of the goods seized is subject to prior lien, the lessor's proceeds may be based only on the interest the tenant actually had in the personal property; any sublessee (undertenant) is liable only to the extent that he owed money to the original tenant.  The seizure of a tenant's property arises from enforcing a *landlord's lien*, which is a statutory right.  The landlord's lien relates back (attaches) to the beginning of the tenancy, not merely to the time the rent became delinquent.

If distress (seizure) of the tenant's property is made for rent justly due the landlord and any irregularity or unlawful act is performed during the distress proceeding by or for the landlord, the tenant may (by legal action) recover for damages from the landlord; however, the act of distress itself is still lawful and the tenant still owes the rent.

If a tenant who has been served with a "pay or quit" notice does pay the arrears before his case comes to trial, he will hold his tenancy just as he did before the proceedings began, without a new lease or conveyance.

In Virginia the confession of judgment clause is legal.  A judgment may be obtained in general district court against a defendant who fails to appear in person or by counsel *if* he is in default and if his lease contained such a clause.  Either the landlord himself or a licensed property manager may actually recover the money awarded in the judgment.

### Rent Control

The General Assembly of Virginia in 1950 declared that the federal rent control is no longer necessary in the state.

### Residential Landlord and Tenant Act

This Virginia statute governs rental of residential property and has the following exemptions:

- Residence at an institution if incidental to detention or the provision of medical, geriatric, educational, counseling, religious or similar services;

- Occupancy under a possession agreement by the purchaser of a property;

- Occupancy by a member of an organization in a portion of a structure operated for the organization;

- Occupancy in a hotel, motel, etc., for not more than a 30-day period;

- Occupancy by an employee of a landlord whose right to occupancy came about from his employment;

- Occupancy by an owner of a condominium unit or holder of a proprietary lease in a cooperative;

- Occupancy under a business, commercial or agricultural lease;

- Occupancy in HUD-regulated housing where such regulation is inconsistent with the act;

- Occupancy by a tenant who pays no rent; and

- Occupancy in single-family residences where the owners are natural persons (or their estates) who own no more than ten single-family residences subject to a rental agreement or, in the case of condominium units, no more than four.

A landlord may require an application fee for tenancy; however, if the fee exceeds $10 and the applicant does not rent the unit, the landlord must return the application fee (except for actual expenses).

## TERMS AND CONDITIONS OF THE RENTAL AGREEMENT

In many aspects of the rental agreement, state law permits great freedom to the parties; however, certain guidelines are specified.

Unless a definite term is set in the lease, the tenancy is construed as week to week for a roomer who pays weekly rent and month to month otherwise.

If the lease permits assignment or subleasing and the prospective assignee or sublessee applies to the landlord in writing (on a form that the landlord should provide), the landlord must approve or disapprove the application within ten days or the application is deemed to have been approved.

A rental agreement, written and delivered by either landlord or tenant to the other party, is in effect whether signed by the other party or not, if the other party does what the agreement requires (i.e., landlord accepts rental payments or tenant proceeds with occupancy and makes rental payments).

### Prohibited Provisions

Virginia law does not permit the following provisions in residential leases:

1.   an agreement to waive rights granted by the act;

2.    a confession of judgment clause (though, as noted earlier, such a clause is legal in nonresidential leases);

3.    an agreement to pay the landlord's attorney fees (with certain exceptions); and

4.    an agreement to limit the landlord's liability to the tenant or indemnify the landlord for the liability or any attendant costs.

Any of these provisions, if included in a residential lease, is unenforceable.

A tenant's records are confidential, except for payment record and the amount of the rental payment. However, someone who is purchasing the rental property has the right to inspect any information the current owner (landlord) has in respect to current or possible tenants. Confidentiality is forfeit when the tenant is default in rent payments.

## Landlord's Obligations

The landlord may not demand a security deposit in excess of two months' rent. He must notify the tenant of any deductions to be made from the deposit in writing and within 30 days of the end of the lease. The landlord must accrue interest in six-month increments at five percent per annum and pay the interest to the tenant at the end of the tenancy; this provision applies only when the lease is for 13 months or more. The landlord must maintain records for each tenant of any deductions made from the security deposit; such records may be inspected by the tenant or his authorized agent.

The landlord must disclose to the tenant, in writing and before the tenancy begins, the name and address of the owner of the property or anyone authorized by him to manage the property or otherwise act in his behalf. If the property is sold, the tenant must be supplied with the name, address and telephone number of the purchaser. If the property is being converted to a condominium or cooperative or the tenant will likely be displaced due to demolition or rehabilitation of the property within the next six months, the tenant is entitled to written notice of the situation.

In maintaining the premises, the landlord must comply with building and housing codes affecting health and safety. He must make repairs to maintain the property in a fit and habitable condition and keep common areas clean and safe. Electrical, plumbing, sanitary, heating, air conditioning and other facilities and appliances supplied by the landlord are to be kept in good and safe working order. The landlord must supply the means for adequate trash removal and must supply running water and reasonable amounts of hot water (except when the hot water is supplied by the tenant or by a direct public utility connection).

In a building where the landlord rents five or more units, the governing body of the municipality may require the landlord to supply locks (cost not to exceed $25 to the tenant) and peepholes (tenant's cost not to exceed $10) within a reasonable time.

## Tenant's Obligations

In addition to the lease provisions, the tenant must keep the premises covered by the lease as clean and safe as conditions permit (including plumbing fixtures), remove garbage and trash and use the facilities and equipment (including heating, plumbing, electrical, sanitary, air conditioning and appliances) in a reasonable manner. He may not through negligence or deliberately deface, destroy or remove any part of the premises or permit anyone else to do so. He must conduct himself in a manner that will not disturb neighbors and abide by all reasonable rules and regulations set down by the landlord.

## Rules and Regulations

A landlord may adopt rules concerning the tenant's use of the premises; rules are enforceable if their purposes are to promote the tenant's welfare and preserve the property, if they are explicit and clear and if the tenant has notice of them from the time of entering into the rental agreement (or from the time of adoption of the rule if later). If a rule is imposed after the tenancy begins, it must not substantially modify the lease without the tenant's written consent.

## Access

The tenant must permit the landlord reasonable access (with landlord giving notice of his intent) to the property to inspect it, to make repairs or alterations as necessary or to show the unit to prospective purchasers or other interested parties. The landlord may enter the unit without the tenant's consent in case of emergency but may not abuse the right of access or harass the tenant. While the tenant may install burglary and fire prevention devices (provided he does not damage the property in doing so), he must supply the landlord or his agent with keys and operating instructions; at the end of the lease, at the landlord's request, the tenant must remove these devices and repair all damages.

At the end of the lease term (or upon default), the tenant must promptly vacate the premises, remove all items of personal property and leave the premises in good clean order.

## Tenant's Remedies

If the landlord violates the rental agreement or fails to comply with the laws regarding health and safety, the tenant may give written notice to the landlord specifying the acts and omissions that constitute the violation and stating that the lease will end at a date not less than 30 days from receipt of the notice, unless the breach is remedied within 21 days. If the landlord remedies the breach, the lease does not terminate. The tenant may not terminate if the violation was brought about by the tenant or his family or anyone on the premises with his consent. If the lease is terminated on account of the noncompliance of the landlord, he must return all security deposits plus accrued interest (if any).

## Military Provision

A member of the U.S. armed forces who is assigned to a new station 50 miles or more from the dwelling unit may terminate the lease by serving the landlord with written notice. This notice must be delivered at least 30 days prior to the termination date it specifies, which date must be no more than 60 days prior to the necessary date of departure. Final rent must be prorated to the termination date; in addition, the landlord may require liquidated damages up to one month's rent if the tenant completes less than six months of the tenancy, or up to one-half month's rent if the tenant completes between six and 12 months' tenancy.

## Fire or Casualty Damage

The Residential Landlord and Tenant Act adds provisions to those already mentioned concerning destruction of premises. If the unit is destroyed or substantially damaged by fire or other casualty, the tenant may immediately vacate the premises and within 14 days give the landlord written notice of intent to terminate the lease, in which case the lease terminates as of the day of vacating. The landlord must return all security deposits and prepaid rent, plus accrued interest.

## Landlord's Noncompliance

The tenant may withhold rent payments from the landlord (paying them instead to the court) if (1) a dangerous condition exists on the premises, (2) the landlord has been notified of it in writing, either by the tenant or by public officials enforcing city health regulations, and (3) the landlord has refused or (even with adequate opportunity) failed to correct the condition. While the court may set a period during which the landlord should take corrective action, Virginia Code specifies that any period in excess of 30 days is too long. If the alleged dangerous condition does not exist or does exist but is brought about by the tenant himself, the landlord may be entitled to damages. However, if the dangerous condition exists and is the landlord's fault and is not corrected within six months, the tenant is entitled to the entire escrow for the six-month period. If the violation still continues, the escrow period begins again, with the same result if the condition remains.

The first court hearing on the tenant's motion against the landlord must be held within 15 days after service of notice on the landlord; however, the court may, on its own motion, order an earlier hearing if an emergency exists (lack of heat in winter, lack of adequate sewage facilities, etc.). The court may hold further hearings to determine compliance with its orders. Escrow monies may be distributed only by order of the court.

## Landlord's Remedies

If the lease is violated, either through nonpayment of rent or through the tenant's dangerous action concerning the premises, the landlord may give the tenant written notice specifying the acts or omissions constituting the breach; the notice states that the lease will terminate not less than 30 days from receipt of the notice if the breach is not remedied within 21 days. If the tenant remedies the breach within the time period specified, the lease does not end. If rent is unpaid, the landlord may serve the tenant with a five-day pay or quit notice; if rent is not paid within the five days, the landlord may terminate the lease and proceed to regain possession of the premises. The landlord may deliver notices to the tenant, or a sheriff may do so upon request, for a fee not to exceed $2.

If the tenant fails to maintain the dwelling as specified in the lease and subsequently fails to have repairs made in a timely manner, the landlord may enter the dwelling and cause the work to be done in a workmanlike manner, submitting an itemized bill to the tenant, to be paid with the next rental payment (or immediately, if the lease has terminated).

The lease may require the tenant to give notice to the landlord of any absence from the leased premises for longer than a week. During any such long absence, the landlord may enter the premises to protect his property. If the tenant abandons the dwelling before the end of the lease, the landlord may rent it to a new tenant, which terminates the earlier lease.

The landlord may not recover possession of leased premises by denying or reducing services or utilities to the tenant or by refusing to permit the tenant access to the unit (unless such refusal is by court order).

If the tenant leaves personal property in the premises after the lease expires, the landlord may consider the items to be abandoned. He must prepare an itemized list of the property and remove the items to a place of safekeeping for one month. During this month the tenant has the right to reclaim the property but must pay reasonable storage and other costs incurred by the landlord. After the 30 days, if the tenant has not reclaimed the property, the landlord may dispose of it as he sees fit. He must keep the itemized list for two years; if he received money for the property, it is applied first to any amounts the tenant owed the landlord (including storage costs); if any funds remain after applying the proceeds in this way, the remaining monies are treated as a security deposit.

### Retaliatory Action

The tenant may bring action against the landlord in several ways (listed below); in such case, the landlord may not retaliate against the tenant by increasing the rent or by decreasing services. Nor may the landlord terminate the lease. The tenant is protected from retaliation if the landlord has notice of any of the following:

1.    The tenant has complained to the government about building code violations or conditions dangerous to health or safety.

2.    The tenant has made a complaint to or filed suit against the landlord for violation of any provision of the Landlord Tenant Act.

3.    The tenant organized or became a member of a tenants' organization

4.    The tenant has testified against the landlord in court.

This provision does not prevent a landlord from increasing his rentals to prevailing market rentals for similar property or from decreasing services that apply equally to all tenants.

### QUESTIONS

1.    Mr. Gressly of Walkup, Virginia, is acting as agent for Mrs. Tombs of Atlanta to receive notices, service of process, etc., for Mrs. Tombs's property in Virginia. Mr. Gressly has been on extended vacation and is nowhere to be found when some notices are served by a tenant. Who will receive these notices?

    a.    The sheriff
    b.    The president of the tenants' association
    c.    Mrs. Tombs
    d.    The Secretary of the Commonwealth

2.    How much notice is required in Virginia for terminating a year-to-year lease if the termination is due to rehabilitation of the property or a change in use?

   a.    30 days
   b.    60 days
   c.    90 days
   d.    120 days

3.    Just before the end of the lease term, tenant Bruckner is injured in an auto crash and spends three weeks in a hospital, during which the lease expires. He sends in the next month's payment, but does not wish to be bound for another year's lease. If the landlord accepts the payment, is Bruckner bound?

   a.    Yes; acceptance means he has another year's lease.
   b.    Yes, though the lease may be shortened by mutual consent.
   c.    No; it was not Bruckner's fault he could not vacate at the end of the term.
   d.    No; all leases automatically become month-to-month if held over.

4.    A tenant rents land and the building thereon. The building is destroyed by fire. Must the tenant still pay rent and abide by all the lease terms?

   a.    Yes; on a ground lease common law so states.
   b.    Yes; such destruction is considered the tenant's fault.
   c.    No; destruction of the improvements terminates a ground lease.
   d.    No; if the tenant is not at fault, he is entitled to rent reduction until his use of the land is restored.

5.    "Distress" as used in leases means:

   a.    seizure of tenant's goods for nonpayment of rent.
   b.    tenant's grievances for noncompliance of landlord.
   c.    landlord's grievance for noncompliance of tenant.
   d.    None of the above

6.    When does a landlord's lien attach to the tenant's property?

   a.    When the tenancy begins
   b.    When delinquency begins
   c.    When five-day notice of pay or quit is served
   d.    When tenancy ends

7.    Which of the following is true of federal rent controls in Virginia?

   a.    They are enforced by the REB.
   b.    They are enforced by local municipal authorities.
   c.    They are self-enforcing until a complaint refers them to HUD.
   d.    They do not exist.

8.   In Virginia, confession of judgment clauses are legal:

     a.   in residential leases only.
     b.   in nonresidential leases only.
     c.   in all leases.
     d.   in no leases.


9.   What is the maximum security deposit the landlord may require?

     a.   $1,000
     b.   One month's rent
     c.   Two months' rent
     d.   The entire rent for the term of the lease


10.  The tenant, concerned for safety, installs a burglar alarm in the premises. Must he inform the landlord?

     a.   No; he has full right of possession during the lease.
     b.   Yes, but he need not supply keys or instructions.
     c.   Yes, but he must give the landlord instructions and keys.
     d.   Yes, for the landlord has unlimited right of access.


11.  Lydia has pointed out to Kent, her landlord, by written notice that bare electric wiring is exposed within her leased apartment. Thirty days have passed, and Kent has done nothing. May Lydia withhold rental payments?

     a.   Yes, if she pays them to the court.
     b.   Yes; Kent has forfeited the right to receive payment.
     c.   No; she must move out first.
     d.   No; she may not withhold rent under any circumstances.

## ANSWERS

1.   d.

2.   d.

3.   c.

4.   d.

5.   a.

6.   a.

7.   d.

8.   b.

9.   c.

10.   c.

11.   a.

# Subdividing and Property Development

This chapter provides a summary of different types of surveys, the requirements for a survey and various Virginia statutes governing the subdivision of property.

## TYPES OF SURVEYS

1.  A *subdivision plat* is a map of each parcel of land showing the subdivided lots, streets, etc. The plat is generally created from a tract of land in order to subdivide it. The subdivided lots may or may not be "staked on the ground" once the plat has been created.

2.  As compared with a subdivision plat, a *boundary survey* shows the boundary or perimeter of the parcel as taken from and applied to the ground, with corner stakes or other physical landmarks shown.

3.  A *house location survey* is a boundary survey with the location of the house shown.

4.  A *physical or as-built survey* is a house location survey with all other physical features of the subject property shown, including water courses, utility lines, fence lines, outbuildings, etc.

A recent recorded survey of a subject property may reveal matters not otherwise reflected in the record. Even though it is primarily the attorney's obligation to examine the survey, the real estate professional, when examining a survey, should look for the following: (1) property boundaries that conform with recorded plat; (2) encroachments by structure onto subject or neighbors' property; (3) fence not on boundary line; (4) party walls; (5) riparian rights of others in streams, lakes, etc.; (6) utilities servicing other properties; (7) old roadways; (8) cemeteries; (9) violation of setback, side or rear building lines; and (10) property that is landlocked.

Any defect shown on the survey should be clearly reported and corrective action taken where necessary.

## REQUIREMENTS OF A SURVEY

Generally, a survey is required in any closing that involves an institutional lender. Further, in a closing where there is owner financing or no requirement for a survey, the real estate professional should recommend that the buyer obtain a survey of the property to be purchased.

Surveys on rural land are of particular importance and may present substantial difficulties. The licensee should realize that such a survey will almost certainly cost more if done in the summer than in the winter, primarily because of visibility and accessibility. In winter, many trees are bare and underbrush has died back, affording a far better view of monuments and landmarks; in addition, insects and dangerous reptiles are less in evidence during the winter. These factors can make a substantial difference where the surveyor is reading and following a metes-and-bounds description with a direction such as "thence north 37 degrees 3 minutes east 2,724.18 feet to a pine." The pine alluded to may be in a pine forest; or it may have been cut down years ago; if the survey is old, it may simply have died. In any event, the surveyor, when traveling through rough country, must attempt to maintain the correct direction and attain the proper distance while fording streams, climbing up and down hills, sidestepping objects (natural or man-made) and attempting to locate himself through whatever other boundaries or monuments may be available. Even when a boundary survey of a large rural property has been done, the surveyor must check for places where his survey might overlap earlier ones or where land might be omitted between parcels. Further, the licensee should be acutely aware that a boundary survey shows nothing concerning improvements or occupancy of the land; he or the owner must check concerning adverse possession or other hostile use of the property.

The survey should meet the following requirements:   (1) It should be prepared and signed by a registered surveyor, with his seal and/or registration number affixed to it.  (2) It should be dated; if it is over six months old, the surveyor shall certify within 90 days of closing that there have been no physical changes since the date last indicated.  (3) It should show dimensions of all lines.  If required, the survey must be compared to the title report prepared by the attorney or title insurance company.  In all cases, the locations and width of all *platted easements* shall be shown on the survey.  Any *easement of substance* recorded by deed or located by book and page shall also be shown on the survey when it is determined that it affects a specific portion of the subject property.  If the surveyor is certain that the easement does not affect the subject property, it must be so stated on the survey.  In both cases, the easement shall be identified by book and page number by the surveyor.  (4) The survey should reflect any fences and setback lines; driveways and joint driveways; the location of all buildings; indicating the distance from the lot line to the main structure; and any encroachments, either of the subject property onto adjacent properties or adjacent properties onto the subject property.  (5) It should show the distance from the intersecting street measured along the same side the street as the subject property.  And, (6) it should reflect the recorded description of subject property and show the address.  The survey must contain the surveyor's certification that there are no encroachments except as shown.

## Plat Maps

In areas using recorded plat maps in lieu of individual surveys, the appropriate lot must be identified and lot dimensions must be legibly shown.  Necessary endorsements to the title insurance policy must be issued pertaining to easements, deed restrictions and property identification.  Endorsements should be obtained by the closing attorney.

## Flood Certification

Flood hazard information may be noted on the survey or by attached statement to the survey if applicable to the area.  Often an institutional lender requires flood insurance coverage if the property is located in a designated flood zone.  If the real estate professional becomes aware that the property is in a designated flood zone, he should notify the attorney and the institutional lender immediately to obtain the necessary insurance prior to closing.

## Encroachments and Easements

Lot dimensions on the survey and/or plat map must agree with those set forth in the FHA, VA or conventional loan appraisal. Any variations must be within allowable limits as set forth in the FHA/VA/FNMA regulations and policy. Any encroachment on the subject property or any adjoining property should be brought to the attention of the lender and the attorney prior to settlement. FHA, VA or a conventional lender may waive certain encroachments, restrictions or limitations on the property. The closing attorney must compare all recorded restrictions, easement and other limitations imposed on the property to those recited in the appraisal and noted in the general waiver provisions of the FHA, VA or FNMA. Notwithstanding these general waiver provisions, the closing attorney, perhaps assisted by the real estate professional, will obtain special waiver letters from FHA, VA or the institutional lender in each of the following cases: (1) an easement involving high pressure gas or oil pipelines; (2) an easement for high power lines; (3) an easement that interferes with the normal or intended use of improvements, including stoops, porches or driveways; (4) Any drainage or irrigation easements; (5) any public utility easement extending more than ten feet from lot line, or the undeterminable location of any easement (easement in gross); (6) any mineral reservation or oil or gas easement or lease; (7) restrictions coupled with a reversion if violated; (8) a property subject to a highway or road right-of-way not contiguous to the lot lines, with title evidence excepting such right-of-way; (9) buildings on adjacent properties that encroach on the subject property more than one foot or any of the subject property's buildings that encroach on adjacent property, with exception of eaves and overhangs encroaching not more than one foot; and (10) restrictions containing a provision that permits any future change in whole or in part within ten years following the date of the loan, and less specific reference to this provision made on the certificate of reasonable value or in the application of certificate of value.

## VIRGINIA STATUTORY REQUIREMENTS FOR SUBDIVISION

The subdivision plat must contain all the necessary approvals of county or city officials and dedications or consents of owners, trustees, etc., and must be properly recorded. Virginia law provides that the recordation of a plat transfer the streets, alleys and other areas set aside for public use to the county or municipality *in fee simple*. The closing attorney should also check to make sure that the subdivision streets have been accepted into the city, county or state system. If the roads are private, it should be determined how they are to be maintained and make sure the buyer knows this. If the roads are to be accepted in the state, county or city systems later, ascertain that a completion or maintenance bond with surety is posted with appropriate authority to assure completion of construction and acceptance by the state, county or city.

## QUESTIONS

1.  If Reynard Fox wishes to verify that the property he is about to buy has no encroachments, setback errors or cemeteries on it, he should check a(n):

    a.  subdivision plat.
    b.  plat of restrictions.
    c.  as-built survey.
    d.  boundary survey.

2.  What is the maximum permissible distance that eaves, overhangs or other improvements on one property may encroach upon another property?

    a.  No encroachment at all
    b.  one foot
    c.  one yard
    d.  No limit if the encroachee obtains a waiver.

3.  The streets, alleys and other areas set aside in a subdivision for public use are transferred to the county or municipality at what point?

    a.  When the subdivision plat is approved
    b.  When the subdivision plat is recorded
    c.  When the streets are completed
    d.  When the streets as completed are approved by the city.

4.  The process or mechanism of transfer of streets in a subdivision to the city is known as:

    a.  eminent domain.
    b.  waiver of ownership.
    c.  conversion
    d.  dedication.

## ANSWERS

1.   c.

2.   b.

3.   b.

4.   d.

# Fair Housing Laws and Ethical Practices

Virginia's fair housing law has been ruled substantially equivalent to the federal fair housing law; accordingly, all complaints under the latter filed from Virginia will be referred to the appropriate enforcement agency in Virginia, which ordinarily is the Virginia Real Estate Board. The fair housing law is considered an exercise of police power within the state. Its essential similarity to the federal statute removes the necessity for exhaustive treatment here: a few minor points only need to be cited.

## EXEMPTIONS

A single-family residence sold by an owner is exempt from the statute, so long as the owner (1) owns no more than three homes at the time, (2) uses no broker or agent and (3) uses no discriminatory advertising. Rooms or units in up to a four-family structure are exempt if the above restrictions are observed and if the owner occupies one of the units.

Church organizations and private clubs, in renting properties that they own, may restrict rentals to their members, so long as membership is not restricted illegally (obviously, the church may discriminate on the basis of religion); again, no broker or salesperson may be used, nor may discriminatory advertising.

It is legal to discriminate on the basis of age to permit all-adult or all-elderly housing or all-elderly sections of a housing community.

It is important to note that (with the exception of the age discrimination referred to in the preceding paragraph) it is illegal for a broker or agent to be involved in discriminatory housing practices in any way. So far as the real estate professional is concerned, THE EXEMPTIONS DO NOT EXIST. They are mentioned here only for the sake of completeness and to provide for the rare cases in which a question concerning the exemptions might arise on a state licensing examination.

Certain restrictive covenants and zoning laws exist that restrict housing in an area to single-family housing. According to Virginia law, a family care home, foster home or group home in which no more than six persons reside who are mentally ill or retarded or developmentally disabled, together with resident counselors or staff, is considered a single-family occupancy.

State-owned or state-supported institutions such as hospitals, nursing homes, schools and correctional institutions may require that persons of both sexes not occupy a single room, unit or dwelling or have to use the same restrooms in the facility.

## REB POWERS

The Real Estate Board has the same powers of conference, conciliation and persuasion given to HUD at the federal level. In addition, if the matter to be resolved involves a real estate licensee, the board has the power to suspend, revoke or deny renewal of a license. The board may subpoena witnesses to testify at its hearings, and the witnesses are interviewed under oath. If a witness does not appear, the board may petition for enforcement of the subpoena in Richmond Circuit Court, where the petition will take precedence over all other cases not otherwise given preference by law.

If the REB has reason to believe that civil action to prevent irreparable harm or to preserve the status quo is warranted, it may advise the attorney general, who may file suit to fulfill the board's purpose.

In any action brought under the Fair Housing Act, the burden of proof is upon the complainant.

## 1988 FAIR HOUSING LAW

The Fair Housing Amendments Act of 1988 strengthens the enforcement mechanisms of earlier laws, while protecting rights of all parties a to jury trial. It extends protection to handicapped persons and to families with children. Thus, fair housing laws now prohibit discrimination on the basis of race, color, religion, sex, national origin, handicap or familial status.

The Department of Housing and Urban Development (HUD) will continue to investigate complaints and to aid in conciliating disputes. HUD must complete its investigation within 100 days of the filing of a complaint. If conciliation fails but HUD determines it is probable that discrimination has occurred or is about to occur, HUD must file a charge against the accused party. Then either party may choose, within 20 days, a trial by jury in federal district court. If this is not done, HUD will pursue the case before an Administrative Law Judge (ALJ), who may award any appropriate relief, including compensatory damages, civil penalties or injunctive relief. Civil penalties would be limited to a maximum of $10,000 for a first offense, $25,000 for a second offense during a five-year period and $50,000 for a third offense during a seven-year period. For those who choose trial before a federal judge, the federal district court can award compensatory or punitive damages and injunctive relief, but not civil penalties. An order by an ALJ can be appealed directly to a federal court of appeals within 30 days; orders of federal district courts may also be appealed.

### Handicapped Individuals

The 1988 law adds handicapped persons to those protected against discrimination and provides a design and construction section to become effective 30 months following the bill's enactment; all other provisions of the bill become effective six months after enactment.

The provision applies to multifamily units in new buildings with elevators and all ground-floor units in new buildings without elevators, but excludes buildings of fewer than four units. The provision requires the following:

1.  Public-use and common-use portions of such dwellings are readily accessible to and usable by handicapped persons.

2.  All doors into and within the premises are wide enough to allow passage by handicapped persons in wheelchairs.

3.  Adaptive designing features must include:

    • an accessible route into and through the building;

    • light switches, electrical outlets, thermostats and other environmental controls in accessible locations;

    • reinforcements in bathroom walls to allow later installation of grab bars; and

    • kitchens and bathrooms usable to a person in a wheelchair.

Usable kitchen and bathroom space does not require a turning radius for wheelchair users; adaptable cabinetry, countertops or special plumbing are not necessary to comply with this bill.

Landlords must allow reasonable modifications to existing units by handicapped occupants at the latter's expense. The definition of handicap does not include illegal use of or addiction to narcotics. The bill protects owners and managers by stating that it does not extend to any individual whose tenancy would constitute a direct threat to the health, safety or property of others.

## Families with Children

The 1988 law protects families with children under 18 years old but provides an exemption for housing for the elderly and near-elderly. Thus, housing occupied exclusively by persons aged 62 or older would be exempt; likewise housing for the near-elderly, defined as that intended for and at least 80 percent occupied by at least one person age 55 or over per unit, would be exempt from the families-with-children provision. To qualify under this category, significant facilities and services must be supplied that are designed for the physical or social needs of older persons. Owners desiring to retain the adult-only character of their properties may convert them to near-elderly status while protecting existing occupants regardless of age. Reasonable local, state or federal restrictions on the maximum number of occupants permitted in a dwelling are not preempted by this bill.

## QUESTIONS

1.  Virginia's fair housing law is considered an exercise of which governmental power?

    a.  Civil rights legislation
    b.  Police power
    c.  Condemnation
    d.  Escheat

2.    An owner may discriminate on the basis of religion in selling or renting his own house in which of the following situations?

      a.    The ad clearly states that religion is a criterion.
      b.    The broker is fully informed of the religion criterion.
      c.    The owner already owns four other properties rented to persons of the same religion.
      d.    None of the above

3.    How do the exemptions to the fair housing law apply with respect to real estate licensees?

      a.    The exemptions do not exist.
      b.    They apply to licensees just as to anyone else.
      c.    They apply when the licensee is giving advice but never in an actual transaction.
      d.    The exemptions apply unless waived by the principals in the transaction.

4.    What are the REB's powers regarding fair housing violations by a licensee?

      a.    Conference, conciliation, persuasion
      b.    Binding arbitration through the local Board of Realtors
      c.    Suspension, revoking or denial of license renewal
      d.    All of the above

5.    The 1988 Fair Housing Amendments Act extended protection against discrimination to which persons or groups?

      a.    Handicapped; drug addicts
      b.    Families with children; handicapped
      c.    Narcotics patients; families with children
      d.    AIDS victims; drug addicts

6.    According to the 1988 act, HUD investigations must be completed how soon after a housing discrimination complaint is filed?

      a.    30 days
      b.    60 days
      c.    100 days
      d.    No statutory limit

7.    HUD's remedies in housing discrimination in the 1988 act were extended to include:

      a.    conference, conciliation, persuasion.
      b.    filing charges, to be adjudicated by an administrative law judge or before a jury in federal district court.
      c.    levying fines of from $10,000 to $50,000 depending upon the number and frequency of the violations.
      d.    awarding compensatory or punitive damages or injunctive relief.

8.   According to the 1988 act, which of the following is now required for handicapped persons in new multifamily buildings?

     a.   Bathroom wall reinforcements for later installation of grab bars
     b.   Elevators
     c.   Thermostats and environmental controls in central locations, easily accessible by building administrators
     d.   All of the above

9.   By the 1988 act, landlords must allow which of the following modifications for handicapped persons to existing rental units?

     a.   Grab bars, accessible outlets and switches, doors wide enough for wheelchairs, all at landlord's expense
     b.   No modifications are called for in existing units
     c.   Any reasonable tenant request, at landlord's expense
     d.   Any reasonable tenant request, at tenant's expense

10.  Janet Hedge is an ex-convict who was injured in an escape from prison where she was serving a sentence for robbery to support her drug habit. She now uses a wheelchair. Janet now wishes to rent a unit in Mr. Daniels' six-unit building. Mr. Daniels has seen Janet's photograph on a wanted poster. What are his obligations as a prospective landlord?

     a.   He must modify doorways to accommodate her wheelchair.
     b.   Because he knows her identity, he must turn her over to the police.
     c.   He must modify her rental space but take measures to protect other tenants.
     d.   Because she is an addict, he has no obligations at all.

11.  The 1988 act provides which exemptions from the law protecting families with children?

     a.   If one or more of the children has AIDS, the landlord need not rent the family a unit.
     b.   If the units already have modifications for the handicapped, the landlord is exempt from having to rent to families with children.
     c.   If the building has already been designated for young couples without children and/or single persons, it is exempt.
     d.   Housing for the elderly or near-elderly is exempt.

12.  How is housing for the elderly defined?

     a.   Units occupied exclusively by persons 62 or older
     b.   80 percent of units occupied by at least one person 55 or older
     c.   Units occupied 100 percent by retired persons, regardless of age
     d.   80 percent of units available to persons 62 or over

## ANSWERS

1.  b.

2.  d.  Exemptions do not apply if discriminatory advertising is used, if a broker or agent is used or if the owner owns more than three homes.

3.  a.

4.  c.

5.  b.

6.  c.

7.  b.  Note that answer c refers to civil penalties not imposed by HUD; answer d refers to court-imposed penalties, also not imposed by HUD.

8.  a.  Elevators would be covered in buildings with more than one floor. The thermostats and other controls would have to be accessible by the handicapped tenant, not the administration.

9.  d.

10. b.  Landlord need not rent to a dangerous person, and narcotics addicts are not a protected class under the law.

11. d.

12. a.  Answer b describes the criteria for near-elderly.

# Closing the Real Estate Transaction

This chapter will focus on the roles of the real estate professional as well as the attorneys for the purchaser and seller in closing a real estate transaction. The purpose of the closing is threefold:

1. The attorneys and the real estate agents explain the closing documents;
2. The parties provide necessary signatures on closing documents; and
3. The attorneys disburse funds after recording the necessary documents.

When all three of these items have been accomplished, the transaction has been consummated.

## PSYCHOLOGICAL ASPECTS OF A CLOSING

For a purchaser and a seller, a real estate closing can evoke a great deal of emotion. The purchasers may be buying their first home and may be excited about the prospects of finally owning a home; however, at the same time, they may be fearful of the closing process and the financial obligations involved with the purchase. The real estate professional must be prepared to deal with almost any type of emotion on the part of the purchaser or seller. In many cases, the agent may not be aware of any particular problem until closing and must be able to adjust quickly to different situations; this takes patience, common sense and sensitivity.

## SUGGESTED PROCEDURE

In order to anticipate problems and minimize those that materialize, the licensee should follow a well-ordered procedure--even using a checklist, if available--to insure the progress of the transaction toward closing. In the ideal situation, during the initial communication the agent will advise the closing attorney of a desired closing date, and both attorney and agent should strive to meet that date. There can be time pressures created by the expiration date of a sales contract or a loan commitment and from the parties who want to close as soon as possible. If problems subsequently develop that are beyond the control of the closing attorney or the real restate agent, all parties should be notified as soon as possible of the delay and reasons for it. Under these circumstances, an extension of the contract might be necessary. It should be noted that unless language to the effect that "time is of the essence" is used the closing date stated in the contract is only a suggested or desired closing date and is not binding upon the parties; failure to close upon such a date will not constitute a default under the contract.

As the closing date draws near, the real estate professional should undertake to review the sales contract, which is the blueprint for the transaction.  Particular attention should be given to the following items:

1.  Correct names of the parties, financial terms and description of property;

2.  Fulfillment of contingencies such as financing, sale of present residence, settlement and possession dates and condition reports;

3.  Clarification of any unclear or ambiguous terms;

4.  Assignment of responsibilities (in fulfilling the terms of the contract) to the attorney, client or real estate agent for such items as obtaining insurance, inspections or financing;

5.  Explanation of costs, fees and expenses (and approximate amounts) and when and how each, together with the purchase price, will be paid--determine how the purchasers will take title and whether the seller agreed to pay any closing costs, points or other charges;

6.  Determine the brokerage commission, any multiple listing service fee and the handling of the deposits; and

7.  Resolve any questions regarding possession (including any necessary possession agreements and their durations and other conditions) and utilities.

Careful planning, communication with the closing attorney and delivery of documents are needed to insure that all required items and information will be available at the closing without creating any delays.

## Survey

If required by either the contract or the loan commitment or if deemed necessary by the title examiner, a survey should be ordered as soon as possible.  The closing attorney normally orders the title examination.  However, if the real estate agent has particular knowledge or information with respect to the survey, this should be communicated to the closing attorney.  It is advisable to provide the surveyor with a copy of a preliminary title report or binder together with a copy of any restrictive covenants, easements or other encumbrances affecting the property known to the sellers.  A completed survey and report should be reviewed and forwarded to the title company, lender, client and the closing attorney.  This should provide adequate time for any encroachments, objections or discrepancies to be addressed.

## Insurance

Generally, a lender requires a hazard insurance policy covering the property securing the loan for a term of one year to be paid prior to or simultaneously with closing.  The different forms of homeowner policies and coverages should be discussed with the buyer, who should be encouraged to contact the insurance agent in order to gain full understanding of the insurance coverage.  The closing attorney or the purchaser traditionally orders the insurance policy and specifies the property description, name of the insured and the wording of the mortgagee "loss payee" clause.  Most lenders require an issued policy and the receipt evidencing payments of the first year's premium as a condition of disbursement of the loan proceeds to the purchaser.

If the property is in a flood zone as determined by the Department of Housing and Urban Development, federal flood insurance will be required on all federally regulated mortgages. Generally, flood insurance can be obtained through the same agent that provides the hazardinsurance policy; however, there is a minimum five-day wait from the time of the application before the issuance of coverage.

## Deed

Generally, the seller's attorney prepares the deed.  The seller's attorney may obtain the information regarding a legal description and the manner in which parties wish to take title by contacting the purchaser's attorney and obtaining a copy of the preliminary title report or by having an independent title search performed in order to ascertain the correct legal description and the manner in which the seller holds the property.  Thereafter, the seller's attorney will usually send a copy of the deed to the purchaser's attorney and have the deed executed by the sellers and notarized either prior to or at the closing.

## Bill of Sale for Personal Property

Where a contract provides for the purchase and sale of personalties, a simple bill of sale with warranty of title and a nonexistence of prior lien should be prepared.  When the title examination is made in a transaction involving the sale of personalty, the index to financing statements should be examined as to the specific property to determine whether liens exist.

## Mechanic's and Materialmen's Lien Waivers

The lien of mechanics or materialmen can, under certain circumstances, take priority over the title of the purchaser as well as the lien of the purchase money deed of trust.  Therefore, certain steps must be taken so that existing liens are extinguished or potential claims waived. In most instances, a title insurance company will routinely accept the seller's affidavit that no repairs or improvements have been made to the property within 120 days of settlement that have not been paid for by the seller.  The title insurance company should be  consulted in advance by the closing attorney as to the form of the affidavit or lien waiver and the extent of coverage provided in the owner's and mortgagee policies.  Generally, the title insurance company will provide a form affidavit regarding mechanics' liens.  Because there generally will have been charges by mechanics or materialmen within 120 days of settlement, it is frequently necessary to obtain a specific lien waiver from each materialmen or mechanic.

## Architectural Control Committee Approval

Frequently, where restrictive covenants are imposed upon a subdivision, an architectural control committee is established to promote orderly and harmonious development.  The specific written approval of the committee should be obtained for the as-built improvements, including all fencing and other exterior improvements.  Generally, it is the obligation of the real estate agent to obtain this information from the architectural control committee and provide it to the closing attorney prior to closing.

## Association Approvals and Membership

Some condominiums, planned unit developments (PUD's), cooperatives and private subdivisions have community associations wherein, by recorded agreement, dues are levied,the nonpayment of which will constitute a lien on the property in Virginia. An estoppel certificate should be obtained from the association indicating that all dues and assessments are current. Such associations may have restrictions covering the alteration of improvements, placing of fences or landscaping. The specific condominium documents should be consulted to insure compliance. Virginia law requires an addendum to be attached to all real estate purchase contracts involving the sale of a condominium that sets forth certain information with respect to the condominium association. Generally the real estate agent obtains this information from the condominium association immediately after the contract is executed and provides this information in the initial submission to the closing attorney.

## Inspections

Frequently a contract will call for a "homebuyers" inspection of various components of the property, such as plumbing, heating, electrical systems, the roof and the foundation. The contract should specify who would pay for any necessary repairs and may set limits of liability to be incurred by either party. The inspections should be ordered promptly and written approval and reports obtained. If exceptions are discovered, the seller's consent should be obtained for repair and arrangements made to see that the work is properly performed and all charges paid.

## Loan Payoffs

A written request should be directed to the holder of any liens discovered by the title examination. It is important to determine the form of payment required, the date for which the payoff figure is good and who will be responsible for the release of the existing lien. A copy of the payoff letter should be delivered to the seller for verification of figures. The real estate agent should provide the closing attorney with information such as the lender or lenders, loan number or other relevant information to assist the closing attorney in obtaining the payoff for any liens on the property. It is also important to note in Virginia that the payoff figures are obtained from and the amount sent to the *noteholder* and not merely the company servicing the loan. Therefore, if the real estate professional knows that the note may have been negotiated or transferred to a party other than the original lender, he should notify the closing attorney of this information. In particular, care should be exercised when ordering a payoff letter involving an FHA loan. (see Chapter 15). The seller should be advised by the real estate agent to continue making regularly scheduled payments until settlement. This will avoid the assessment of late charges and the reporting of the account as being delinquent. The seller should be able to provide either receipts or canceled checks of such payments in the event they have not been verified to the purchaser's attorney by the lender. As a general rule, the closing attorney cannot deviate from the payoff letter furnished to the attorney by the lender. Therefore, if a recent payment is not reflected on the payoff letter, this may have to be worked out between the seller and the lender to be paid off after closing.

## Leases

If the property is a rental property, for example a duplex, the nature and terms of the tenancy should be determined and reviewed. Rents should be prorated, security deposits (together with all accrued interest) transferred and tenants notified.  It is traditionally the real estate agent's obligation to assist the closing attorney in ascertaining information regarding rental of the property.

## Possession

Frequently, the contract warrants that possession is to be delivered at the closing.  However, if possession will not coincide with closing, written understanding should be reached regarding such matters as risk of loss, liability, utilities, compensation and delivery of possession.

Typically, when a seller is allowed to remain in the premises after closing has taken place, a possession agreement is entered into and the rent is set at a figure mutually agreeable to the parties.  Often the seller will agree to pay an amount equal to the monthly payment of the principal, interest, taxes and insurance paid by the purchaser/owner.

On occasion the purchaser may move into the property prior to the closing.  As a practical matter, this can create problems in that the purchaser usually finds certain things that need to be corrected or repaired that were not covered by the contract or not detected during the homebuyer's inspection.  This may cause delay in the closing or perhaps cause the closing to fall through altogether.

## Title Examination and Title Insurance

Title should be promptly examined and a preliminary report prepared.  If objections or defects are discovered, these should be reported to the seller's attorney and a resolution sought.  Frequently minor defects will be insured by a title company as a matter of underwriting.  The title report should be reviewed with the client and all exceptions, easements and restrictions explained.  The lender should likewise receive and approve the title report.  Virtually all commercial lenders require title insurance for their protection only.  The purchaser should be advised of the differences in cost coverage between owner and mortgagee policies.  Frequently a purchaser will be entitled to a reissue rate at a substantially reduced premium if the owner of the property has previously secured an owner's policy.  The real estate agent in almost all circumstances should advise the purchaser to obtain owner's as well as lender's title insurance.  The premium is nominal as compared to the cost associated with any claim made against the title.

On occasion, the title report may reveal a deed of trust against the property that is not released in the land records but that the seller states has been paid.  Frequently this is the result of the closing attorney in a prior transaction not having a certificate of satisfaction or release recorded.  The real estate agent may be called upon to assist the closing attorney in obtaining a certificate of satisfaction from the former closing attorney or other parties, stating that the obligation has been paid off.

## Document Preparation

The closing documents are generally prepared by the closing attorney on forms furnished by the lender.  Generally the real estate agent is not called upon to prepare any forms, but occasionally may be asked to assist the closing attorney in obtaining and delivering a termite report, contract addendum or other documentation.

## Payment Authorization

The approval of all parties should be obtained as to exactly what will and will not be paid by the closing attorney. If the sale proceeds are to be paid to anyone other than the seller, specific written authorization should be obtained.

## "Walk Through" Inspections

The seller and/or the lender may require the purchaser to inspect and accept the property immediately prior to closing. If defects are discovered, a written understanding should be reached as soon as possible regarding the remedy of any such defect or monies to be withheld in escrow until repairs are complete.

## Termite Report

Frequently a seller must furnish a purchaser with a report that the property is free from damage by termites or other wood destroying insects. However, if infestation or damage is found, the premises should be treated or repaired and the work guaranteed at the seller's expense.

## New Construction

In transactions involving new construction, an itemized list of any extra charges should be obtained and an agreement reached as to amounts of the payment. Any changes should be handled through change orders, with additional charges specified and agreed to at that time. The real estate agent, particularly a site agent on new construction, should provide this information to the closing attorney. A certificate of occupancy as well as evidence of payment of any sewer, water or other utility connection charges should be obtained.

## Lender's Approval

Copies of the entire loan package should be delivered to the lender in advance of closing and its instructions obtained concerning both the form and substance of all documents. Generally, delivering the package to the lender is the role of the closing attorney. The real estate agent may wish to monitor the approval process of the loan itself but need not monitor the approval of the final package, since this is the role of the closing attorney.

## Closing Statements

Virtually all residential real estate transactions involving new loans are now governed by the Real Estate Settlement Procedures Act (RESPA), which requires the use of Form HUD-1 as a settlement statement.

## Proration

Arrangements should be made to secure the financial information on each item to be prorated or adjusted between the purchaser and seller. Frequently adjusted items are (1) oil, (2) rent,

(3) association dues, (4) real estate taxes, (5) insurance premiums, and (6) escrows.  Generally, the real estate agent is responsible for obtaining information on items 1 through 3 above, whereas the closing attorney is responsible for obtaining information on 4 through 6.  In practice, the closing attorney may obtain information on all of the above.

## The Closing

Several days before the closing, the parties should be contacted and a specific time and place for closing agreed upon.  The purchaser should be advised who must be present to execute the required documents.  Frequently the buyers and sellers, any real estate agents and the buyer's and seller's respective attorneys will be present at closing.  Closing usually takes place at the office of the buyer's attorney.  The purchaser must be advised to have the needed funds in the form of cash, a cashier's or certified check, or a wire transfer.  A closing attorney cannot disburse uncollected funds; therefore, a personal check is usually not acceptable.
Arrangements should be made, often through the real estate agent handling the transaction, to have all utilities transferred (*not* discontinued) from the name of the seller to that of the purchaser on the date of settlement.  The seller or real estate agent should deliver, along with the deed and other closing documents, all keys and operating instructions for any equipment or appliances.  Following the closing, a purchaser may be well advised to have all locks changed or tumblers reset.  Generally, the seller's counsel will have delivered the deed and other seller's documents in escrow.  At closing, the purchaser will sign all documents required by the contract and the lender will tender the funds required to settle.  The purchaser should receive both an explanation and a copy of each of the settlement documents.  If the financing documents provide for adjustable rates, balloon payments or prohibitions against assumptions, a full explanation should be given to the purchaser by the closing attorney.  Before the purchaser leaves the settlement, each document should be checked by the closing attorney for proper signatures, dates and acknowledgements.

## Recordation and Disbursement

Title to the property should be continued down from the date of the preliminary report of title to the moment the papers are filed of record.  If no objections are discovered, the deed following any deed of trust is tendered for recording.  If a new exception appears, documents will not be recorded until the issue is resolved.  The executed note, a conformed copy of the deed of trust, gross recording receipt and other required loan documents should be delivered promptly to the lender.  Most lenders also require a written statement that each of the requirements set forth in the loan commitment and the title insurance commitment have been fulfilled, the deed of trust has been recorded, and no new objections of record have appeared.  All funds should be promptly disbursed in accordance with the settlement statement.  Under the Wet Settlement Act in Virginia, lenders are required to make prompt disbursements of loan proceeds from immediately available funds drawn on an institution within the fifth federal reserve district, and the settlement agent must disburse the settlement proceeds within two business days of settlement.  Unless written authorization has been received to the contrary, all proceeds checks should be made jointly to all of the sellers.  It should be noted that no settlement proceeds may be disbursed prior to recordation of the deed of trust or other documents creating a security interest in favor of the lender in the property.

## QUESTIONS

1.   Purpose(s) of closing include which of the following?

   a.   Explaining documents to participants
   b.   Obtaining signatures as needed on documents
   c.   Disbursement of funds to those entitled to receive them
   d.   All of the above


2.   Which of the following is true of the closing date stated in a sales contract?

   a.   It is fixed and binding on the parties.
   b.   It is binding if "time is of the essence."
   c.   It is not binding.
   d.   It is binding only if specified in the listing as well.


3.   Garfin, salesperson for Helms Realty, discovers after all parties had signed a sales
     contract for the purchase by assumption of his listing that his client's garden fence, built
     30 years ago, encroaches on the property of his neighbor to the rear.  What should
     Garfin do?

   a.   Notify seller and closing attorney immediately.
   b.   Call a contractor and have the fence moved.
   c.   Nothing:  the encroachment has been there long enough to be an easement by
        prescription.
   d.   Recommend that the buyer avoid the expense of a survey, which is not mandatory
        on an assumption.


4.   If personal property conveys with the real property, what sort of document transfers it to
     the buyer?

   a.   Personalty deed
   b.   Bill of sale
   c.   Deposit receipt
   d.   The same deed that conveys the real property


5.   The seller's affidavit that no repairs or improvements have been made on the property
     covers what time period?

   a.   Five business days
   b.   30 days
   c.   90 days
   d.   120 days

6. How should the real estate licensee verify that the seller's PUD fees are paid up and current?

   a. Ask the seller.
   b. Have the seller sign an affidavit to the effect.
   c. Obtain an estoppel certificate from the PUD association.
   d. Since this would show up in the title search, the licensee has no responsibility in this matter.

7. What is required by the Wet Settlement Act in Virginia?

   a. No funds can be disbursed on waterfront property without approval of the local Wetlands Board.
   b. No funds can be disbursed after closing till all necessary documents have been recorded.
   c. No documents can be recorded until all proper funds have been disbursed.
   d. The attorneys must sign and record an affidavit to the effect that all funds have been disbursed and all documents recorded.

## ANSWERS

1.   d.

2.   b.   Normal language states that settlement will be held on or before (date) or as soon afterward as title can be cleared and papers prepared. It is not a firm date unless a "time is of the essence" clause make it so.

3.   a.   All parties must be notified. While a survey is not mandatory on an assumption, it is highly advisable, especially if a problem appears. The encroachment might, indeed, be of long enough standing to constitute an easement by prescription; even so, all parties are entitled to know of it.

4.   b.

5.   d.

6.   c.

7.   b.

# Index

# More Real Estate Books That Help You Get Ahead

## 15-DAY FREE EXAMINATION ORDER CARD

810060

Please send me the books I have
indicated. I'll receive a refund with
no further obligation for any books I
return within the 15-day period.

□ Please send me your latest catalog.
□ Please send me more information on the
Longman Investor Bookshelf.

**Real Estate Education Company**
a division of
**Longman Financial Services Institute, Inc.**
520 North Dearborn Street
Chicago, Illinois 60610-4975

NAME _____

ADDRESS _____

CITY/STATE/ZIP _____

TELEPHONE( ) _____

## TEXTBOOKS

| | | Order # | | Price | Total Amount |
|---|---|---|---|---|---|
| □ | 1. | 1970-04 | Questions & Answers to Help You Pass the Real Estate Exam, 3rd ed. | $21.95 | _____ |
| □ | 2. | 1970-02 | Guide to Passing the Real Estate Exam (ACT), 3rd ed. | $21.95 | _____ |
| □ | 3. | 1970-01 | The Real Estate Education Company Exam Manual, 4th ed. (ETS) | $19.95 | _____ |
| □ | 4. | 1970-06 | Real Estate Exam Guide (ASI), 2nd ed. | $21.95 | _____ |
| □ | 5. | 1970-03 | How to Prepare for the Texas Real Estate Exam, 3rd ed. | $19.95 | _____ |
| □ | 6. | 1556-10 | Fundamentals of Real Estate Appraisal, 4th ed. | $34.95 | _____ |
| □ | 7. | 1557-10 | Essentials of Real Estate Finance, 5th ed. | $38.95 | _____ |
| □ | 8. | 1559-01 | Essentials of Real Estate Investment, 3rd ed. | $34.95 | _____ |
| □ | 9. | 1513-01 | Real Estate Fundamentals, 3rd ed. | $22.95 | _____ |
| □ | 10. | 1551-10 | Property Management, 3rd ed. | $34.95 | _____ |
| □ | 11. | 1560-01 | Real Estate Law, 2nd ed. | $38.95 | _____ |
| □ | 12. | 1965-01 | Real Estate Brokerage: A Success Guide, 2nd ed. | $35.95 | _____ |
| □ | 13. | 1510-01 | Modern Real Estate Practice, 11th ed. | $32.95 | _____ |
| □ | 14. | 1510- | Supplements for Modern Real Estate Practice are available for many states. Indicate the state you're interested in _____ | $10.95 | _____ |
| □ | 15. | 1510-02 | Modern Real Estate Practice Study Guide, 11th ed. | $13.95 | _____ |
| □ | 16. | 1961-01 | The Language of Real Estate, 3rd ed. | $26.95 | _____ |
| □ | 17. | 1512-10 | Mastering Real Estate Mathematics, 5th ed. | $25.95 | _____ |
| □ | 18. | 1560-08 | Agency Relationships in Real Estate | $24.95 | _____ |

## PROFESSIONAL BOOKS

| | | | | Price | |
|---|---|---|---|---|---|
| □ | 19. | 1913-01 | List for Success | $18.95 | _____ |
| □ | 20. | 1913-04 | Close for Success | $18.95 | _____ |
| □ | 21. | 1913-06 | The Complete Homebuyer's Kit | $14.95 | _____ |
| □ | 22. | 1927-03 | Fast Start in Real Estate: A Survival Guide for New Agents | $17.95 | _____ |
| □ | 23. | 1926-01 | Classified Secrets, 2nd ed. | $29.95 | _____ |
| □ | 24. | 1907-01 | Power Real Estate Listing, 2nd ed. | $16.95 | _____ |
| □ | 25. | 1907-02 | Power Real Estate Selling, 2nd ed. | $16.95 | _____ |
| □ | 26. | 5606-24 | The Mortgage Kit | $14.95 | _____ |
| □ | 27. | 4105-07 | How to Profit from Real Estate | $19.95 | _____ |
| □ | 28. | 4105-06 | How to Sell Apartment Buildings | $19.95 | _____ |
| □ | 29. | 4105-08 | Landlord's Handbook | $19.95 | _____ |
| □ | 30. | 1913-05 | The Complete Homeseller's Kit | $14.95 | _____ |
| □ | 31. | 1909-01 | New Home Sales | $24.95 | _____ |
| □ | 32. | 1909-03 | New Home Marketing | $34.95 | _____ |
| □ | 33. | 1922-02 | Successful Leasing and Selling of Office Property, 3rd. ed. | $34.95 | _____ |
| □ | 34. | 1922-01 | Successful Industrial Real Estate Brokerage, 4th ed. | $34.95 | _____ |
| □ | 35. | 1978-02 | The Recruiting Revolution in Real Estate | $34.95 | _____ |
| □ | 36. | 1922-03 | Successful Leasing and Selling of Retail Property, 3rd ed. | $34.95 | _____ |

**Book Total** _____

## PAYMENT MUST ACCOMPANY ALL ORDERS:
(check one)

□ Check or money order payable to
  Real Estate Education Company
□ Charge to my credit card
  (circle one) **VISA** or **MasterCard** or **AMEX**

Account No. _____ Exp. date _____

Signature _____

ALL CHARGE ORDERS MUST BE SIGNED.

**Or call toll-free 1-800-621-9621, ext. 650;**
**In Illinois, 1-800-654-8596, ext. 650 (charge orders only)**

Also available at your local bookstore.

Orders shipped to the following states
must include applicable sales tax:
AZ, CA, CO, IL, MI, MN,
NJ, NY, PA, TX, VA and WI.

_____

**Add postage and handling**
(see chart)          _____

**Total** _____

| TOTAL BOOK PURCHASE | SHIPPING & HANDLING CHARGES |
|---|---|
| $ 00.00- 24.99 | $ 4.00 |
| $ 25.00- 49.99 | 5.00 |
| $ 50.00- 99.99 | 6.00 |
| $100.00-249.99 | 8.00 |
| $250.00 and over | 11.00 |

PRICES SUBJECT TO CHANGE WITHOUT NOTICE

Real Estate Education Company

**LONGMAN**
WHERE EXPERTS BEGIN

# REAL ESTATE EDUCATION COMPANY

## PROPERTY MANAGEMENT, 3rd Edition,

by Robert C. Kyle, with Floyd M. Baird, RPA/SMA, Contributing Editor

The revised third edition presents management techniques for apartment buildings, co-ops, condominiums, office buildings, and commercial and industrial properties. Includes steps for creating a management plan and discussions of how to handle owner/tenant relations, leasing procedures, marketing space, and other problems. *Property Management's* popular, practical approach to management is enhanced by numerous sample forms, ads, and charts.

Key features added to the third edition:
* discussion of single family homes—how they differ from apartments, vacation homes, and timeshare properties
* section on trust relationships
* coverage of the ''intelligent building,'' including maintenance of automation systems, telecommunications, and office automation
* discussion of industrial development incentives, including industrial revenue bonds, foreign trade zones, and others

**Check box #10 on the order card.     $34.95     Order Number 1551-10     copyright 1988**

---

## ESSENTIALS OF REAL ESTATE INVESTMENT, 3rd Edition,

by David Sirota

Completely updated and reorganized, the third edition provides the most timely treatment available of an area of real estate that is constantly changing. Effects of the 1986 Tax Reform Act on the real estate investment process and its applications are fully explained.

Third edition highlights include:
* financing and insurance topics consolidated into one chapter
* additional discussion of defaults and foreclosures
* updated coverage of S Corporations—*vis-a-vis* the Subchapter S Revision Act and 1986 Tax Reform Act
* explanation of how the Uniform Partnership Act controls partnerships

**Check box #8 on the order card.     $34.95     Order Number 1559-01     copyright 1988**

---

## REAL ESTATE BROKERAGE: A SUCCESS GUIDE, 2nd Edition,

by John E. Cyr and Joan m. Sobeck

Newly published in its second edition, this text sets the industry standard on opening and operating a real estate brokerage office. Revised and updated to reflect today's market, it features coverage of such timely topics as agency and the effects of the 1986 Tax Reform Act. Also included is a new chapter focusing on industry trends.

Key features of the second edition include:
* presentation of agency and the law
* discussion of one-appointment approach to obtaining listings (in addition to two-appointment method)
* changes resulting from the 1986 Tax Reform Act—revised income tax deductions related to brokers' expenses, effects on investor ownership, depreciation, maintenance, refinancing, and installment sales
* glossary

**Check box #12 on the order card.     $35.95     Order Number 1965-01     copyright 1988**

---

## AGENCY RELATIONSHIPS IN REAL ESTATE

By John W. Reilly

This timely book explains all of the real estate agent's basic relationships with buyers and sellers of real estate—including the hot topic of ''dual agency''—in clearly written, nontechnical language. The text also fully discusses kinds of services offered to clients, as opposed to customers, as well as types of agency representation a broker may choose to offer. Practical information on how to avoid misrepresentations is also presented.

*Agency Relationships in Real Estate* features:
* extensive appendix on all U.S. cases involving agency
* in-text situations and examples that highlight and emphasize key points
* checklists that show the agent's responsibilities and obligations
* quiz and discussion questions that reinforce important concepts

**Check box #18 on order card     $24.95     Order Number 1560-08     copyright 1987**

 Real Estate Education Co.

LONGMAN
WHERE EXPERTS BEGIN